GOOD
HOUSEKEEPING

SIMPLE ORGANIZING WISDOM

GOOD HOUSEKEEPING

SIMPLE ORGANIZING WISDOM

500+ QUICK & EASY CLUTTER CURES

EDITED BY LAURIE JENNINGS

HEARST
books

2

18

56

84

112

140

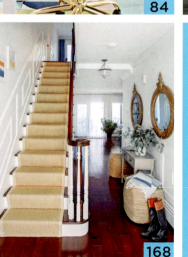

168

CONTENTS

LET'S GET ORGANIZING!

Okay, are you with me? If you're holding this book in your hands, I'm guessing yes! And I couldn't be more excited to share *Good Housekeeping*'s best organizing tips and expert tricks with you in this pretty, inspiring, easy-to-use book.

With chapters dedicated to every room in your home (plus your car and backyard!), *Good Housekeeping Simple Organizing Wisdom* is a go-to resource to help you tackle your toughest storage and straightening problems. So whether you're dealing with limited closet space, a too-small bathroom, or not enough laundry-room shelving, you'll find simple solutions to help you maximize every single inch, wall-to-wall and floor-to-ceiling.

The best part is every chapter is broken out into smaller projects, so you won't feel like you have to take on everything all at once. We set you up for success from the very beginning with useful advice like our 9 Daily Must-Do's to Stay Organized Forever and The Must List, our guide to the 15 most essential organizing gadgets. Then we dive right into most people's biggest problem area: the kitchen. You'll learn how to streamline everything from the fridge and pantry to cupboards, drawers, and cookware. From there, we've got great strategies to make your living, sleeping, and home office spaces work harder than ever yet feel more beautiful all at the same time. Even utility zones like your mudroom, laundry room, and basement will look more inviting and functional.

Of course it wouldn't be *Good Housekeeping* if we didn't also offer up top-tested product picks from the experts in the Good Housekeeping Institute and feature items that carry the Good Housekeeping Seal—the most trusted third-party consumer emblem for over 100 years and the only one that comes with a two-year limited warranty!

I've always admired people who have a lean and streamlined home, where there's a place for everything and everything is in its place. And I'm sure you agree, it feels great to walk through the front door and be greeted by a perfectly pristine scene—especially when it's yours.

Happy organizing!

—Laurie Jennings
Director
Good Housekeeping Institute

MAXIMIZE A CORNER

Nestle a bistro table and chairs in front
of a built-in bench to create a casual spot
to catch up with loved ones when the
organizing is done.

ORGANIZING ESSENTIALS

No professional organizer can get by without a label maker, and neither should you. It's a home organizer's secret weapon—along with the other 14 must-have products and double-duty life savers found in this chapter. So if you want to keep your home clutter-free forever, it's time to stock up on our curated lists of essential tools and space-making solutions. We've also added time-saving ideas, important mistakes to avoid, and even a planning calendar—so you can stay on track, now and every day forward!

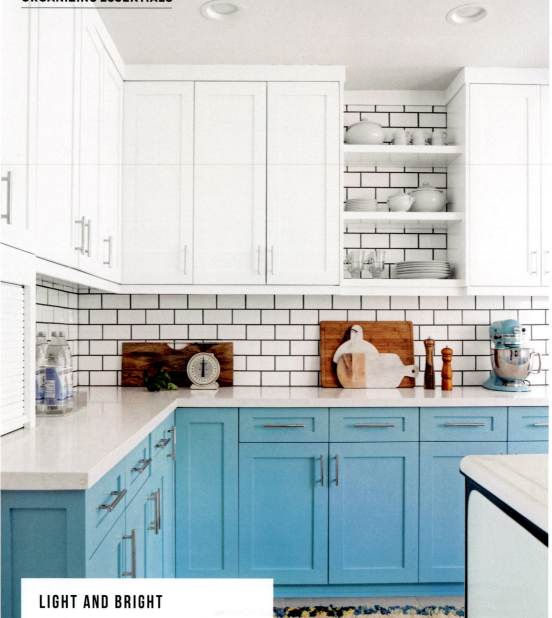

LIGHT AND BRIGHT

You don't have to commit to floor-to-ceiling color to get a space that looks balanced and inviting. Leave the upper portion white and add an energetic hue below.

GETTING STARTED

Follow these five key strategies to kick off decluttering and optimize your organizing effort.

DON'T GET OVERWHELMED

Sure, it looks like you have a lot to do, but don't let the size of the task make you throw in the towel right from the start. Break large jobs into smaller ones, and don't tackle more than you can accomplish in the time you have available. Keep your eyes on the prize and have the confidence that it will all get done. Because it will!

MAKE A LIST

Walk through your home and prioritize the areas most in need of organizing help. Start with the obvious messes. The satisfaction of cleaning up a cluttered space that's been annoying you is well worth the effort and will give you the inspiration you'll need for the rest of the tasks that follow. Itemize within each area too, so you can cross off mini accomplishments as you make them.

SHOP FOR ORGANIZERS

Take some time to peruse the aisles or websites of home and organizing stores to see what new and innovative storage boxes, bins, caddies, and racks are on the market—and make sure to check out our Must List on the following pages. This will give you ideas about cool tools available to make better use of your space. Browse social media sites like Pinterest® and Instagram® to get inspiration from how others organize and the creative ways they solve common clutter problems.

DECIDE WHERE TO DONATE

Research charities or organizations that will accept your items or find out how to dispose of or recycle things that can't be donated. Make arrangements to get rid of things as soon as you collect them. Many services will pick up as little as one bag of clothing. This way you're not creating more clutter as items to be donated or tossed pile up.

DELEGATE

You didn't clutter up your house by yourself, so you shouldn't have to clean it up alone. Involve kids or a spouse, partner, or roommate in the process and even let them choose what decluttering jobs they'd most like to do. Be prepared to give some guidance and suggestions, then let them take ownership of the task and feel the sense of accomplishment when it's complete. They'll also be more likely to keep an area organized when they have a vested interest in it. Everyone wins!

GROCERY LIST:

COFFEE
JELLY
MILK
cake flour
ARUGULA
QUINOA
cereal
almonds
KALE
paper towels

9 DAILY MUST-DO'S TO STAY ORGANIZED FOREVER

Perform these simple tasks every day, and clutter
will never get the better of you again!

1 WRITE OUT A TO-DO LIST. Take a few minutes in the morning to jot down your goals for the day. Having a concrete list will keep you on track and give you a sense of accomplishment as each task is completed.

2 MAKE THE BED. Bed-making promotes productivity throughout the day and will pave the way to an organized lifestyle. And there's no reason kids can't be taught from an early age to make their own beds. Plus, it's a pleasure to get into a neatly made bed at the end of a long day.

3 TEND TO CLOTHING AS SOON AS YOU TAKE IT OFF. Hang, launder, or fold every garment, and don't let anything hit the floor. Neglected clothing can slowly build up until it has created an overwhelming mound.

4 DEAL WITH THE DISHES. A sink full of cups and plates will make your entire kitchen look and feel messy. Get into the habit of loading the dishwasher and washing dishes at the end of the day, or at least soak the dishes so you can quickly wash them the next day.

5 WIPE DOWN SURFACES. Your counters inevitably get dirty every day, so take a minute or two to wipe them before you head to bed.

6 SORT THROUGH THE MAIL. Tend to your mailbox daily to avoid a buildup of bills and to-do's. Immediately toss junk mail into the recycling bin or shredder, and store the rest in an active inbox so it will stay on your radar.

7 ALWAYS PUT KEYS IN THE SAME SPOT. Whether it's a hook by the front door or a catchall near the entrance, make sure your keys have a clear destination. You don't want to spend time searching for them when you need them.

8 EMPTY POCKETS AND BAGS AT DAY'S END. Take a couple of minutes to throw away any trash you've acquired during the day. Place loose change in your wallet or a coin jar and make sure any loose papers are filed, shredded, recycled, or thrown away.

9 PLAN FOR TOMORROW. Before heading to bed, mentally walk through the next day and do your best to prepare for it. Set aside necessary items, plan your outfit, and pack your bag so you can grab it on the fly.

BEST DOUBLE-DUTY ORGANIZERS

Nothing is more rewarding than finding a new use for something you already own, and we found many. Happy repurposing!

MAGAZINE FILE

Flip this office staple on its side to create the perfect home for a stack of cans that might otherwise hog or fall off pantry shelves. It also helps you fit more cans in less shelf space.

EYEGLASSES CASE

Snag a spare case to store jewelry when packing a suitcase or to hold earbuds and digital chargers and cables so you can find them in a hurry. The hard shell protects what's inside.

SPICE RACK

Mount long, horizontal trays designed to hold spices in your bathroom, and nail polishes and makeup tools will always be within reach. In your child's room, they can put books on display.

GARMENT BAG

Wrapping-paper rolls never seem to stay upright and inevitably topple as you go to grab one. Store them vertically in a plastic garment bag. A clear one is best, but even one you got the last time you bought a coat would work. Then just hang it in a closet, and everything is contained.

POT LID RACK

Borrow this handy organizer from your kitchen to keep clutches, wallets, even sunglasses cases upright and orderly on your bedroom closet shelf.

MASON JAR

Often used to store dry ingredients and other nonperishables in the pantry, a lidded mason jar is a great place to store other baking supplies, like cupcake liners. Use mini ones in the office for paper clips or pushpins, too.

HANGING FRUIT BASKET

Rubber duckies and other bath toys aren't so cute when you're constantly tripping over them in the tub or on the bathroom floor. Hang a tiered wire fruit basket from the shower curtain rod to give playthings a permanent home. The wire design also allows toys to dry.

PILLBOX

This organizer's tiny compartments keep your smallest earrings, rings, and pins safe at home and while you're traveling. Put a different item in each of the Sunday-through-Saturday labeled compartments.

COAT HOOKS

Mount a row or two of coat hooks near the floor in your mudroom, and suddenly that pile of shoes turns into neatly hung rows of footwear.

WINE RACK

Those wall-mounted wine racks that hold bottles horizontally are perfect for storing extra bathroom or kitchen hand towels so they are always at the ready. Simply roll each towel tightly and slip it into a slot.

STANDING COAT RACK

Move this from your front foyer to the bedroom and hang totes and purses from it so they won't get crushed on your closet shelf and will stay in view.

BAR CART

Organize books, stuffed animals, and even towels and toiletries on a mini three-tier kitchen trolley cart. The best part is that you can wheel or stash it wherever you want it.

DRESSER DRAWER

Before you haul an old piece of furniture out to the curb, consider repurposing the drawers as under-the-bed storage bins. Add wheels to make access even easier, and cover items to keep them clean.

PILLOWCASE

When storing coats or special-occasion clothing, cover each item with a clean old pillowcase. Cut a small hole in the sewn end and slip the case over the hanger. It breathes and won't hold mildew-causing moisture like plastic does.

PANTS HANGER

A pants hanger makes a great jewelry hanger and can slip right into your closet. Thread bracelets and necklaces onto the rungs, and when you want to access a piece of jewelry, simply pivot out the appropriate bar or slip it off the open end.

PAPER PLATE

Tuck it between stacks of nonstick pans in your cabinet to keep them scratch-free, or in a stored cast-iron pan to absorb moisture. Use it to cover food you are reheating in the microwave, too. It offers more protection than a paper towel, and your microwave will stay cleaner.

YOUR DECLUTTERING CALENDAR

Follow this easy checklist from our GH Institute home care experts to get sorted today, tomorrow, and beyond!

DAILY

KITCHEN
- Empty the sink every night (hand-wash dishes or run the dishwasher) and close cabinet doors.
- Remove clutter on counters. Put away food, pots and pans, and small appliances.

BATHROOM
- Straighten towels and washcloths.
- Check that shampoo, conditioner, etc., are organized in a shower caddy or put away.
- Make sure hair tools, skin-care products, and makeup are properly stored.

BEDROOM
- Make beds every morning. An unmade bed is like an invitation to be messy.
- Put away clothing and other items.
- Every night, as part of a bedtime ritual, have your child put toys into bins or other receptacles.

OFFICE & WORKROOM
- Go through the daily inbox of mail; handle, shred, or recycle.
- Avoid accidents: Store sharp tools like scissors.

GARAGE & SHEDS
- Place like items in close proximity (group together all sports gear, pet supplies, etc.).

WEEKLY

KITCHEN
- Monitor the kitchen or dining table: Put things that don't belong on it into a bin every night. Once a week, the family member who has the most items in the bin has to put everything away.

BEDROOM
- Do a weekly visual sweep of the bed and the surrounding area and remove anything out of place.
- Change bed linens.
- Check the nightstand to see that it's neat and organized.
- If your kids can't walk directly to their beds from the door, they need to put away whatever is in their path.
- Reorganize garments by type if they've gotten mixed up.

FOYER/ENTRYWAY
- Rehang coats that have fallen and rearrange if needed.
- Place shoes and boots so they are easily accessible.

OFFICE & WORKROOM
- Take a few minutes to return everything to its rightful place so you can work with a clear mind.

GARAGE & SHEDS
- Make sure recycling bins are not overflowing. If they are, replace them with larger, or more, containers.

OCCASIONALLY

KITCHEN
- Thoroughly clean cabinets and drawers.
- Empty the fridge: Remove and discard items that are past their prime. Place the oldest items in the front.

BATHROOM
- Restock shampoo, toilet paper, etc., as needed.
- Discard meds that are past their expiration date.

BEDROOM
- Once a month do a drawer check and straightening.
- Donate (or sell) items in the closet you don't wear.
- Place all hangers facing one direction at the start of the season. Once you've worn an item, face the hanger the opposite way.

OFFICE & CRAFT ROOM
- Order paper, ink cartridges, and anything that's running low.
- Go through files and archive what you don't need.

ATTIC & BASEMENT
- Every three months, examine emergency supplies to confirm that batteries are still good, equipment is functioning, and food and beverages aren't leaking, damaged, or expired.

7 ORGANIZING MISTAKES TO STOP MAKING

These are the bad habits professional organizers
wish we'd break once and for all.

1 YOU PUT PAPER CLUTTER INTO NEAT PILES. Stacking mail and receipts doesn't reduce the quantity of papers; it just rearranges them. Instead, use hanging files to separate papers into actionable categories. This will make it easier for you to see what you need to tackle now and what you need to allot time for in the future.

2 YOU HOARD GROCERY BAGS. Yes, it's convenient to have bags at the ready for life's messy moments. However, holding on to too many is unnecessary. Instead, keep one larger bag to hold all the other bags and don't keep more than can fit within it, or buy a grocery-bag dispenser and mount it inside a cabinet door.

3 YOU STASH STUFF OUT OF SIGHT. You've heard it before: "Out of sight, out of mind." But if you follow this rule, chances are you're holding on to items you don't need and, worse, don't know you have. Even if you have space to store everything, what's the point in keeping it? Your space should be filled with items that you actually use.

4 YOU DON'T PUT THINGS BACK. Scissors are used in many rooms, which means if you forget to put them away, they can be impossible to find. After something's been used, it must go back to its home. This eliminates lost items and acquiring duplicates of things you already own.

5 YOU WON'T PART WITH UNWANTED ITEMS. The salt and pepper shakers your mother-in-law gave you might be adorable, but if they're not to your taste, you should part with them. Keeping an item that you don't like just because someone gave it to you adds to the clutter. If you are concerned about hurt feelings, let a little time pass and then quietly donate it.

6 YOU HAVE TOO MANY OPEN SHELVES. While candles, photos, and pretty kitchenware are lovely to display, open shelves can get very messy very quickly, and the items on them will need frequent cleaning. And things like personal-care products are best kept under wraps. Limit open shelving, and use it only for items you don't access often.

7 YOU VIEW ORGANIZING AS A ONE-TIME EVENT. After sending half your closet off to Goodwill, give yourself a pat on the back. But organizing should be done regularly. Choose products and systems that work with your lifestyle, your home's design, and your family. You'll be more likely to stick with them.

THE MUST LIST

These are the 15 space-savers all professional organizers have in their arsenal.

1 PEGBOARD. Add one to your garage or mudroom to keep tools or gardening supplies corralled. For extra organization, once items have "homes," trace them with permanent marker so you'll always know where things go—and if something is missing.

2 STACKABLE DRAWERS. Available in a range of sizes, these are perfect for keeping your under-the-sink area organized or adding extra storage to closets. But don't feel you must keep them hidden behind closed doors! They also come in a variety of styles that look great on display in a home office or den. Best of all, it's easy to add more drawers as you need!

3 WICKER AND WOVEN BASKETS. Use these as a chic place to store soft goods, like towels or extra linens—roll them for an organized, pretty display.

4 SEE-THROUGH BINS. Ideal for corralling things like art supplies, these come in tons of sizes to keep your stuff together and easily visible.

5 COLORFUL BOXES. Great for anything you want to keep out of sight. Grab a matching set or opt for an assortment of shades for a fun pop of color.

6 PAPER SHREDDER. Get rid of clutter instantly and securely with an at-home shredder that makes quick work of junk mail, old receipts, and more.

7 SHOE ORGANIZER. Ditch the pile of mismatched shoes and replace it with an easy under-the-bed or over-the-door organizer. They'll keep your kicks together and help them look newer, longer.

8 GLASS JARS/CONTAINERS. Turn your pantry into Pinterest goals with streamlined glass jars. Use them to hold baking goods like flour and sugar, pastas, and rice, and even to ditch unsightly cereal boxes.

9 DRAWER ORGANIZERS. Avoid the dreaded junk drawer effect by adding handy inserts inside drawers throughout your house. Smaller sections mean less time searching for that special pen or favorite lipstick and helps keep you from randomly throwing things in.

10 SHELVES. For extra storage, all you have to do is look up! Add shelves to your walls to maximize space and display hidden-away photos or pretty trinkets.

11 TRAYS. From metallic to wood to acrylic, grab a few of these to turn cluttered areas (like your coffee table or vanity) into chic, curated displays.

12 LABEL MAKER. The holy grail of organizing gadgets, this handy tool is perfect for remembering what goes where and what belongs to whom.

13 HOOKS. Hang a bunch throughout the house to keep coats, purses, and keys neat and easy to reach. If you're a renter or don't want to damage walls, opt for adhesive, removable ones instead.

14 CORKBOARD. Not just a place to keep old photos or aced assignments, create a "home hub" where you can exchange notes with family members. Use them in the bedroom to hang necklaces, the office to display a calendar, or the pantry.

15 BINDER CLIPS. The ultimate do-it-all helper, use these as stand-ins for chip clips or to create an organized charging station. Attach clips to the edge of a table and thread the ends of the cord through them.

POPS OF COLOR

Swap traditional dark wood stools for a rainbow set of metal seats. In an all-white kitchen, they're a refreshing and easy way to show your personality while keeping the overall look ordered and sleek. Pull it all together by choosing a single shade for other countertop accessories.

KITCHEN + PANTRY

Welcome to command central. From cooking to working to gathering with family and friends, your kitchen is the place in your home where life happens. So, it's no surprise that clutter here leads to clutter everywhere. And we can't have that! That's why this chapter is fully loaded with simple, practical solutions to maximize space without compromising style. Follow our expert advice to streamline everything—the counters, pantry, even that dreaded cupboard under the kitchen sink—and give yourself back time and stress-relieving sanity.

Discreet cabinets for max storage!

SUPER STORAGE

From your cabinets to your island, aim for a mix of hidden and open storage. This provides the greatest versatility to tuck away frequently used items, like food wrap and serving dishes, but also allows you to show off items like a beloved stand mixer or a treasured cookbook collection. Max out the functionality of your island by opting for discreet cupboards on both sides and creating a breakfast bar on one side.

GOING CLEAR

Consider glass-panel upper cabinets to show off dinnerware collections, vintage finds, or heirloom pieces. Group items by color or function to keep things neat and design a cohesive display. Plus, it's easier to put them away! Use glass mason jars to store dry goods or corral cutlery and cooking utensils.

SAVED BY THE BIN

Fill the bottom shelf of an island or open shelves with a series of large woven baskets to stash everything from newspapers to produce. Unfinished butcher-block shelves add levels of easy-access storage.

PRO ORGANIZER
TIPS TO STEAL

Use these strategies to create the ultimate streamlined space,
where there's a place for everything and everything is in its place!

1 OPT FOR WHITE. This timeless, crisp neutral provides a fresh and clean backdrop for the hardest-working room in your home. A simple white color scheme helps eliminate visual clutter and allows chic touches like stainless steel appliances or bright cookware to stand out. Consider it for some of the most permanent features, like cabinets or counters.

2 PUT MONEY IN THE DETAILS. High-end touches—like brass pulls on cabinetry and a marble mosaic backsplash—stand out, elevating everything around them. Or for a truly sleek look, skip cabinets and drawer pulls altogether. Some cabinet manufacturers offer a new push-pull mechanism that allows you to open drawers and cupboards with a gentle touch.

3 STRATEGICALLY SET THE TABLE. Like countertops, the kitchen (or dining) table can easily become a dumping ground for . . . everything! Avoid this trap by keeping tables "set" with placemats or a table runner and a fruit bowl or vase. Family members will be less likely to drop items there. Here's a quick tip: Choose easy-to-clean fabrics like cotton or linen for your table coverings, and wash immediately after use to keep them looking fresh.

4 ROLL OUT A RUG. Add stylish texture (and comfort!) underfoot by laying down a cozy rug in your main work zone. Opt for a graphic pattern that will hide drips and spills more easily—and help tie the room together. Use a rug pad to keep it from slipping and sliding.

5 COMPARTMENTALIZE. Use a variety of trays and drawer dividers to neatly corral kitchen gadgets. An in-drawer knife block keeps blades sharp—and out of the reach of kids. Shelf inserts keep dinnerware and glasses neatly stowed.

6 CAMOUFLAGE YOUR TRASH. Disguise less attractive contents, like compost or recycling, in opaque receptacles with labels on the outside. Or retrofit a large pull-out drawer with built-in bins.

7 MAKE IT ALL SPARKLE. Wipe away spills, crumbs, and grease splatters with a multi-purpose spray cleaner and a cloth or sponge well-wrung in hot water. For any stuck-on bits, use a scrub sponge dipped in baking soda. Shine up stainless steel appliances to remove fingerprints and streaks.

ALL THINGS VISIBLE

Freestanding shelves are simpler (and less pricey) to install than cabinets, and give a breezy, casual feel to a kitchen. Open, slide-out shelves make it easy to access cooking gear in wicker baskets.

CLEAR OFF THE COUNTERS

Open, uncluttered spaces look cleaner than those piled high. Jumbles of stuff can give the impression that a room is messy and dirty, even when it's not. Designate one drawer or bin for mail and papers, and set aside time each week to open and file must-keep items. Place rarely used small appliances, like a juicer or a waffle maker, in upper cupboards or out-of-the-way closets. Voilà! You just scored loads of valuable workspace.

STACK YOUR SHELVES

Replace cabinets with open shelving. This visually expands a small kitchen and offers easy access to dishware. For drawers and lower cabinets, fake a fancy custom look with a fresh coat of paint in an eye-catching hue, like blue here.

BUILD A BANQUETTE

In an eat-in kitchen, make the most of
a corner—and a spectacular view—by
installing an L-shaped banquette. Add
hinges to the seating for bonus easy-access
storage below. Top it with custom-sized
cushions and cozy throw pillows.

REINVENT THE KITCHEN TABLE

Prep, serve, and entertain on a multi-purpose butcher-block island with stools that fit underneath, offering plenty of seating for a gathering of friends or family. When the party is over, tuck in the stools to open up the room's flow.

STYLE YOUR WALLS

Wooden cutting boards and silver platters are much too pretty to hide inside cabinets. Instead, hang them from hooks or lean them against the wall in an artful arrangement—and make them part of your decor! Create less visual clutter by opting for a slide-in range (with knobs on the front and no back panel) that sits flush with the counter.

FANTASTIC FRIDGE

Innovative smart-home technology is exploding when it comes to refrigerators. This Miele® model makes food last longer and taste fresher thanks to special sensors that deliver expert temperature and humidity control.

8 RULES FOR A WELL-ORDERED FRIDGE

Never lose a bag of carrots in the bottom of the crisper again. Here's how to keep this kitchen powerhouse fresh and organized.

1 PURGE OFTEN. Pull over the trash can and dump leftovers, spoiled food, and old condiments. Wipe shelves, bins, and the front door and handles with a wet cloth or sponge. Wipe the bottoms of jars and packages before returning them inside.

2 STRETCH OUT SHELF SPACE. Stash food in stackable, square storage containers rather than round ones—the square shape lets you store more food and keeps things neat. Instead of placing leftovers in huge containers, stow them as individual portions in smaller bins or resealable bags for grab-and-go meals.

3 GROUP POPULAR COMBOS IN BINS. Place like items—such as deli meat, cheeses, and condiments—together in see-through bins to make them easier to access. Plus, you won't have to go to the fridge multiple times or bundle things in your arms when prepping meals.

4 PUT GROCERIES IN THE RIGHT PLACE. Stow produce in crisper drawers and store snack items, like cheese sticks and hummus packs, together in the deli drawer. Items will fit better and create more usable space. Keep perishables (like eggs) in their original packaging so you can track expiration dates.

5 AVOID OVERCROWDING. Don't let unopened cans of soda and single-serve bottles of iced tea crowd food that must be kept cold. Instead, store shelf-stable bottles and cans in the pantry and cool them down with ice when you need them.

6 STORE PERISHABLES SO THEY LAST. Double-bag raw meat and place on a platter on the bottom shelf to avoid leaks that could contaminate other fresh foods. Pat wet fruits and veggies with a dry paper towel before placing inside the crisper.

7 USE THE FREEZER TO SAVE ROOM. Freeze milk in its container (it will keep for up to three months) and thaw it in the refrigerator. Chop herbs and mix with a teaspoon or two of olive oil. Put in a resealable bag, removing all the air and marking the bag so you know what's inside, and freeze so the mixture lies flat. Break off pieces to season soups and sauces. Or use an ice cube tray to freeze individual portions.

8 LABEL ZONES. There will be lots of hands in your fridge. Create a road map and label "zones" with stickers for things like beverages and leftovers. That way, when searching for appetizers during a party or meal prepping, you'll know where everything is.

1-MINUTE TIP! **Keep odors in check.** Forgotten food stuck way in the back can create unpleasant smells that can transfer to other foods and even ice. Place a fresh box of baking soda inside your fridge every three months to help erase any stink. Use tight-sealing storage containers, like Snapware® Total Solution™ Pyrex Glass Containers, to keep leftovers from going bad.

7 SNEAKY WAYS TO GAIN EXTRA COUNTER SPACE

If it seems like you never have enough of this valuable kitchen real estate, here's how to reclaim some room.

1 MAKE THREE PILES. Label the piles always used, seldom used, and never used. Toss or donate anything that ends up in the last group.

2 BANISH THE UTENSIL JAR. You use only one or two utensils at a time, so why let your entire collection eat up valuable counter space? Instead, hang your favorites inside a nearby cabinet door.

3 CORRAL LIKE WITH LIKE. Line often-used spices together along the back of your range and group cooking oils and seasonings on a butcher block.

4 GO BIG. Choose an island that is large enough for the kitchen so you can have much-needed additional counter space.

5 TRY A MOVABLE ISLAND. If you don't have room for a permanent island or need a slightly bigger one, consider a rolling unit on wheels. Pull it out when you need it and stash it in a corner when you don't.

6 ADD ANOTHER LEVEL. If you have open wall space and prefer to keep your most frequently used items out and visible, add a shelf between your counter and the upper cabinets. Depending on the space, it can hold spices, small dishes, books, and more.

7 DON'T FORGET ABOUT YOUR BACKSPLASH. Hanging baskets from towels bars mounted to the wall can contain condiments, baking essentials, even a decorative plant. Use hooks to hang gadgets, colanders, and cookware.

CAESARSTONE® COUNTERS

This ultra-resistant countertop material, made from 93 percent quartz and 7 percent polyester resin, is scratch-, heat-, and mildew-resistant. It's ideal for kitchens and bathrooms. Plus, it's super-tough and easier to clean than granite—and always looks new, even years after installation.

5 TRICKS FOR MAKING ROOM IN CABINETS & DRAWERS

The more your cabinets can hold, the more orderly your kitchen looks. Time to get them working harder!

1 TURN ONE SHELF INTO TWO. Use wire shelf risers to take full advantage of all vertical storage space inside cupboards that was once wasted by tough-to-stack items, like teapots and cups.

2 EXTEND CABINETS TO THE CEILING. Run your upper cupboards the full height of the room. Or if the space isn't high enough, place baskets on top of cabinets to hold items like cookbooks, vases, or other important but seldom-used entertaining essentials.

3 SHOW BOXES THE DOOR. Keep plastic wrap, parchment paper, and aluminum foil both within reach and out of the way by stowing them in a well-hidden magazine file attached to the inside of a cupboard door. Choose a cupboard adjacent to your food prep area.

4 BE NARROW-MINDED. Install a slim, pull-out cabinet in the skinny, wasted space between your fridge and the wall. Use this prime real estate for organizing canned goods. Pretty it up by adding a decorative handle and peel-and-stick wallpaper behind shelves (which will also make it easier to clean).

5 SHIP OUT THE SEASONAL STUFF. No need to let your ice cream maker or corn-on-the-cob holders take up space in the dead of winter. Same goes for holiday cookie cutters or that seldom-used fondue set during a summer heat wave. Group similar items together, then pack them up and move them to a designated spot in your garage or basement during the off-season.

1-MINUTE TIP! **Put things away.** Quickly survey the scene in your kitchen. Find a home for any appliances that have been left out on the counter to collect dust. If your hand-washed dishes are drying on a rack, take a towel to them if necessary, then put them away. Choose a dish rack or drainer that rolls or folds up for easy storage when not in use.

ADD "DRAWERS"
TO DEEP CABINETS

Store everything from table linens to toys in durable plastic bins. They are easy to pull out so you won't have to dig for stuff way in the back.

STORE PANS ON THEIR SIDES

Use an adjustable pan rack to vertically store pots and pans. This stops them from getting jumbled inside a cupboard and makes it easier to see (and grab!) the cookware you need.

TRY A LAZY SUSAN

This versatile space-saver is especially helpful in corners and other hard-to-reach areas. Use it in cabinets to hold spices and cleaning supplies (and also in the refrigerator or pantry to corral condiments, snacks, and more). Some are two-tiered for extra storage. Look for easy-clean plastic and nonslip grips to keep items from falling.

SHED SOME LIGHT

Consider adding battery-operated, motion-sensor LED lights inside dark or hard-to-reach cabinets like the one under the sink or above the refrigerator. Look for lights that stick on, which can be installed in a second.

Copper pieces make a pretty display.

ADD MORE STORAGE

A big island can house a sink, numerous storage cabinets, and a below-counter-height oven-and-microwave combo (saving valuable counter space) under a broad work surface.

HANG IT UP

Take advantage of the empty wall space above a cooktop or stove to install a sturdy metal rack for pots and pans. Not only does this sneaky trick put frequently used cookware in easy reach, it frees up space inside cupboards and drawers to maximize storage. Just be sure each item hangs freely—about three pieces is perfect.

CONQUER COOKWARE CLUTTER

Discover how to wrangle these awkward pieces once and for all.

USE SPACE OVERHEAD

If you're lucky enough to have high ceilings in your kitchen, reclaim your "air rights" by suspending a hanging pot rack from the ceiling above an island. Whether you choose to mix or match metals, it's an ideal solution to score more space inside cupboards and drawers.

GET SOME HOOKS

Attach hooks, like damage-free ones from Command® to exposed cabinet, island, or wall spaces to hang lightweight pans so they're handy. Nest heavy pieces in lower cabinets with paper plates or shelf liners inside to prevent scratches. Corral lids on door-mounted racks.

DIVIDE A DEEP DRAWER

Add ¼-inch pieces of plywood to your deepest drawer to divide the larger space, create cubbies for all your pots and pans, and avoid epic stacking fails.

MOVE THEM TO THE PANTRY

If you have a walk-in pantry (lucky you!), make the most of the back wall by hanging your bulky kitchen accessories on it. Now items are quick and easy to find, use, and store.

TRY A PEGBOARD

A bare, blank wall gets a stylish (and functional!) upgrade with a black pegboard. Hang your pots and pans from hooks and outline them in chalk so you never forget where each item lives.

WHAT TO KEEP, WHAT TO TOSS

Some well-worn cookware just needs a little love—and some are a lost cause. Here's how to know the difference.

KEEP

- **Pot lids with missing knobs.** If the pan or pot is still in working order, contact the manufacturer for the replacement part. If the knob has merely become detached and you still have it, take it—together with the lid—to your local hardware store to buy a replacement screw. For a tighter fit, add a washer just below the screw head.

- **Discolored stainless steel.** Caused by high heat, the blueish tint won't affect performance. Scrub it with a specifically formulated product, like Cameo Stainless Steel Cleaner, to remove discoloration. Bonus: It takes off brown grease splatters, too.

TOSS

- **Mismatched lids.** If the pots are long gone, why save the tops? They are doing nothing inside your cupboard but taking up space and collecting dust.

- **Warped baking pans.** If you use these, baked goods will come out misshapen and may cook unevenly. Next time, let hot baking pans cool before soaking them in the sink (thermal shock causes that warping).

- **Overflowing plastic containers and lids.** It's tempting to save all those takeaway containers and other plastic tubs from yogurt or margarine, but fight that urge. Just get rid of them. Replace them with a certified dishwasher- and microwave-safe set.

THE ONLY COOKWARE YOU REALLY NEED

You can toss or donate everything else. We promise.

FOR DAY-TO-DAY COOKING

- Three skillets (8-, 10-, and 12-inch)
- Two saucepans (2- and 4-quart)
- One 6-quart Dutch oven
- One 8-quart stockpot

FOR BAKING AND ROASTING

- Two cookie sheets
- Two 9-inch round cake pans
- One 8-inch-square brownie pan
- One 13 × 9-inch roasting pan
- One 9-inch glass pie plate

STREAMLINE THE SINK

This busy zone handles cooking, cleanup, and more. Here's how to keep it tidy and ready for action when you need it.

AVOID DIRTY DISH PILEUPS

Load stray items into the dishwasher immediately after use. Rinse and wipe drippy detergent bottles and relocate extra scrubbers, brushes, and rubber gloves under the sink. De-gunk the hand soap dispenser with a hot water rinse, and wipe the faucet and surrounding area of any water that's splashed.

CLEAR NEARBY COUNTERS

Mount a paper towel holder inside an under-sink cabinet door to free up counter space. Attach a clothespin to clip rubber gloves out of sight. Small door baskets can keep scrubbers and brushes from cluttering your sink top.

TRY TOWEL BARS

Simple chrome rods on runners or hinges mounted to the inside of your cabinet doors are a great way to hide kitchen towels while still keeping them accessible. Even pot holders can be looped onto one of the rods.

SANITIZE SPONGES

Nothing destroys the look of a sink area more than a grimy, smelly sponge, not to mention the germs it spreads. Clean yours every few days with a five-minute soak in a mix of three tablespoons of chlorine bleach and one quart of water. You can also zap germs by putting the sponge, saturated with water, in the microwave for one or two minutes. Replace sponges when they start to fall apart. If you use dishcloths, launder them often in hot water with bleach.

STASH TRASH

If your under-sink cabinet is big enough, look for dual bins mounted on smooth runners or pullout tracks to hold small garbage and recycling pails. This will keep these messy pileups out of sight. Just remember to empty them daily or when filled.

CLEAN AND DRY THE SINK

Germs grow wherever there is water and food, so clean the sink daily with a bleach or germ-killing cleanser. Pay special attention to the faucet handles and drain. Dry the area when you are done.

3 TRICKS TO ORGANIZING UNDER THE SINK

It's all about sorting through the clutter and preserving cabinet space.

1 PULL OUT YOUR CLEANING SUPPLIES and toss anything that is dried out or used up. Arrange the remaining cleansers by room or type (e.g., bathroom, dusting) and place each group in a plastic bin— they'll be easy to relocate or grab at chore time.

2 SAVE THE ROOM UNDER YOUR KITCHEN SINK for the supplies you use in and around your kitchen— dish-cleaning supplies, all-purpose cleaner, stainless steel polish, trash bags, etc. Ideally, keep other cleaners, like bathroom and window solutions, in another location.

3 LINE THE FLOOR OF AN UNDER-SINK CABINET with inexpensive vinyl tiles or shelf liner for easy cleaning when spills or drips happen. Use bins and door-mounted hooks or clothespins to organize and give cloths, brushes, scrubbers, and rubber gloves a place to dry after use.

ORDER SPICES

Line the inside of a cupboard door with slim shelves, then go A-to-Z, so everything is alphabetized and easy to find. Or, if you're more task-oriented, group herbs and spices by use. Designate one shelf for baking and include extracts, cinnamon, baking powder, and baking soda.

PLAN THE PERFECT PANTRY

Start by pulling everything out. Then follow these steps
to fight the mess—and bring order back—in no time!

1 SORT YOUR GOODS. Create categories (baking ingredients, seasoning and spices, dry grains) and group them together before you restock the shelves.

2 PAY ATTENTION TO EXPIRATION DATES. While everything is still out, check for expired items and products that look moldy, dusty, or generally inedible. Throw away open boxes of food that are more than six months old. Move older cans to the front when restocking.

3 PLACE DAILY-USE ESSENTIALS FRONT AND CENTER. Stow daily-use items, like cereal and dog food, in the easiest zone to access: in-between waist and eye level. Store extras on the bottom and occasional-use items on higher shelves.

4 CHOOSE CLEAR CONTAINERS. See-through canisters and storage containers let you know what you have on hand and will save you an extra trip to the store.

5 USE PROPER STORAGE CONTAINERS. Make sure cereal stays fresh and chips remain crispy by using the best container for each specific purpose (see Storage Container Smarts, page 51).

6 RETHINK BUYING IN BULK. The lost shelf space may negate the savings if it takes a year to get through extra-large purchases. One solution: Transfer portions into smaller containers and stash the extras up high. Or perhaps buddy up with a neighbor or friend to get the price break with less stuff to store.

7 AVOID TURNING THE PANTRY INTO A DUMPING GROUND. Keep an eye on things like tools and cleaning supplies—some aren't safe to store near food! Remove non–food-related items and keep them out.

8 WEED OUT THINGS YOU'VE FORGOTTEN. Get rid of any ingredients or gadgets you haven't used in a year or two (so long, panini press). Toss or donate them.

STORAGE CONTAINER SMARTS

Whether you need to store flour or dry pasta, match the perfect storage solution to its specific purpose—and rely on our picks, which scored high in airtightness, leakproofness, and other rigorous kitchen appliances tests.

GLASS CONTAINERS

These are the most airtight option if the lids latch securely. They also reheat well in the microwave or oven (double-check the marks on the bottom). But they are breakable, so be careful when using them on the go.

Try: EMSA by Frieling™ Clip & Close Glass Containers

DRY-GOODS CANISTERS

With their gasket-sealed lids, these handy vessels keep air from infiltrating loose pasta, flour, rice, sugar, nuts, oatmeal, dried beans, and other basics. Steel or glass options protect pantry staples better than porous ceramic—and they're often pretty enough to sit on a counter (just don't go overboard). Push down the lid to force air out.

Try: Prepara® Evak Storage Containers

RESEALABLE PLASTIC POUCHES

Bags take up less room than containers. Though not 100 percent airtight, they work well for cereal, veggies, and foods you use often and want to keep crisp.

Try: BlueAvocado® (Re)zip Reusable Storage Bags

TAKE-ALONG CHOICE

These plastic containers have removable ice packs for lunchtime perishables like tuna salad and fruit. The lids snap onto the bottom so they won't get lost.

Try: Snapware Total Solution Plastic On-the-Go Sets

Q: HOW OFTEN CAN I REUSE A FOOD STORAGE CONTAINER?

A: Not all containers are food-safe a second time. Glass jars clean easily for refilling with sauces, salad dressings, soups, and more. But margarine/dairy tubs and takeout containers aren't dishwasher safe and can even degrade if hand-washed. Resealable plastic bags can harbor bacteria, so don't simply rinse and reuse.

WiFi: 6f2fe8z

olive oil
trash bags
stamps

*renew
license!

DIY COMMUNICATION STATION

How to handle the daily onslaught of kids' permission slips, bills, and junk mail.

GIVE EVERYONE HIS OR HER OWN SLOT

To keep track of your family's messages and mail, set up a wall-mounted magazine rack and designate a slot for each family member.

PEN IT IN

A color-coded calendar (with a different hue for each person) will keep the crew on schedule. But don't write everything here—save personal activities for your own datebook or e-calendar. Just jot down events that involve multiple family members (say things that require a driver).

PIN IT UP

Put up a bulletin board where everyone can see it, and use pushpins to attach flyers, invites, and tickets. Tack an envelope to the bulletin board to stash coupons, gift certificates, or other cards you might need to grab on your way out the door. This way you'll be able to move coupons from the mail bin into the envelope.

WRITE IT OUT

Consider a chalkboard or a dry-erase board for handwritten notes to yourself.

CLIP IT

A clipboard or zippered pouch will let you take papers or mail with you so you can tackle them while waiting in the carpool line or at the doctor's office.

TOSS ONE THING

Each time you add an item to your bin, get rid of one, too. When you've got this much coming in, it's easy for papers (and whatever else) to pile up. Purge your bulletin board of no-longer-needed papers when you change the calendar page.

STASH THE TRASH

Keep a garbage can or recycling bin nearby (or, even better, a paper shredder) for all the papers you've dealt with—or already know are junk. When possible, sign up for online opt-outs, like electronic billing.

TAKE ADVANTAGE OF E-REMINDERS

Unlike pesky paper, a digital note is hard to lose. Use online shared calendars (such as GoogleCal), send invites for the kids' recitals, or text yourself the grocery list.

SORT SMARTER

Stop mail clutter in a bin with three sections: IN, OUT, and READ. IN is for mail that needs to be dealt with weekly (bills, paperwork, etc.); OUT is for outgoing mail; READ is for materials to peruse later (magazines, newsletters, etc., to be purged monthly). Kids' paperwork for you goes in the IN box; once handled, move it to their magazine-rack slots.

MAKE NOTES

A sticky note on the door is the perfect can't-miss-it reminder. Tuck the notepad and pen in a bin (near your station) meant for holding outgoing items like those library books that are due tomorrow.

EAT

8 TRICKS TO MAKE YOUR KITCHEN MORE ORGANIZED FOR KIDS

And, as a result, make your life way easier, too.

1 BUILD A KIDDIE CORNER. Create a kitchen-based art-and-play station to keep little hands occupied during meal prep. Hang an ultra-organized wall unit for essential supplies, like markers and coloring pencils. Use extra pockets for bills and letters.

2 DEDICATE A DRAWER. If you want your kiddos to learn how to fend for themselves (and then pick up afterwards, too!), choose one drawer to store all their stuff. That way they never have to ask you where things belong before taking initiative.

3 KEEP DRINKING GLASSES WITHIN REACH. Now this is what we call an excellent use of magnets: Attach them to the backs of plastic cups, and stick the cups on the fridge door, so a drink is always available. Just make sure your kiddos don't stick a full glass of juice or water back on the door when they're done sipping (hello, spills galore).

4 MAKE A CEREAL STATION. When you put single servings of cereal in a drawer and a milk dispenser in the fridge, your kids won't have to wake you up on Saturday morning for breakfast. Let them watch cartoons while you get an extra hour of sleep.

5 START A SNACK BASKET. In your pantry, set aside baggies of snacks for your kids so they can grab 'em (once they get the go-ahead from you, of course). Keep a drawer in your fridge for cheese sticks and fruit, too.

6 ASSIGN CUPS TO EACH LITTLE ONE. Stop letting your kids' thirst rule your life. Instead, hang cups near the water dispenser in different colors, so your children can grab their dedicated glass without having to tell you a thing.

7 GO MINI. Kids love to "cook" and "bake" at their own stovetop. Outfit one shelf with miniature appliances and cooking tools and supplies. Stock it with fruits and veggies or a tea or coffee set. Encourage kids to keep their cabinets organized, too.

8 INVOLVE THEM. If you store all your cereal bowls in one low drawer, your kids can be in charge of unloading these items while you're unpacking the dishwasher. Plus, this means they'll always know where to look for the bowls in the morning (win-win).

GO FOR GOOD FLOW

Try to include at least one round piece,
such as a coffee table, that people can
walk around without bumping their knees.
Also add a versatile piece, like a garden
stool, that can be used as a stool
to sit on or as a table for a drink.

LIVING + FAMILY ROOMS

Mastering the mess of your home's primary lounging zones is no easy feat. Kids' toys, endless remotes, and various souvenirs (read: junk) from the day seem to have a magnetic pull to these living spaces, but defying this force is easier than you think. Whether you have an hour or even five minutes, we're here to offer fast fixes for even the most high-traffic space.

SAVVY STORAGE

Frame a window with built-in bookcases that combine shelves on top and cupboards on the bottom. Use the space under the window for a bench.

Show off pieces from your travels.

GROUP ART SHOW

Arrange pottery and glassware in recessed nooks over a built-in desk. Grouping similar items creates a sophisticated, stylish, uncluttered focal point.

PRO ORGANIZER TIPS TO STEAL

Try these quick clutter fixes to keep your family's living spaces mess-free.

DARE TO BE SPARE

Ease living room congestion by sticking to the basics—a sofa, one or two comfy chairs, a coffee table—and arranging them for clear, unimpeded traffic flow.

CREATE BALANCE

Establish a sense of equilibrium by using matching side tables and table lamps on either side of your couch. Finish the look with graphic drapes.

DOUBLE UP

Use pieces that serve multiple functions, like an ottoman that works as both spare seating and hidden storage, or furniture pieces that combine a mix of drawers and shelves.

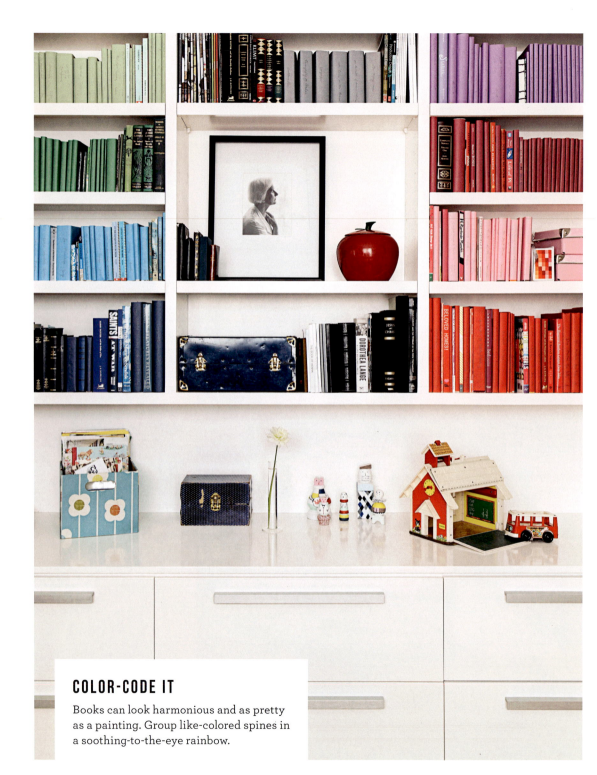

COLOR-CODE IT

Books can look harmonious and as pretty
as a painting. Group like-colored spines in
a soothing-to-the-eye rainbow.

Lean a mirror on a shelf and you won't damage the wall.

PAIR SOME SIDE TABLES

Save space—and increase flexibility—with two smaller tables. Place them in front of the fireplace for extra seating or use them instead of a traditional coffee table.

SET UP A SWEET SEAT

Take advantage of an unused nook by transforming it into a little seating area, perfect for morning coffee or reading. Look for a small-profile couch (often called a settee) to fill the space just right.

CREATE VIGNETTES

Turn the fireplace into an artful focal point for all your things. On the mantel, mix pieces of art with candlesticks and decorative boxes. When grouping items, vary shapes, sizes, and colors for the most distinctive display. A giant basket is perfect to store logs for the fire.

ANCHOR THE TV

Place a mixed-purpose chest below a wall-mounted TV to achieve a balanced look. Accessorize the top of the chest with a large bowl, stack of books, and family portraits. Conceal other electronics on the shelves below.

UNDER COVER

An oversize pine trunk doubles as the
perfect hidden living room storage spot.
Big, cushy upholstery looks even cozier
when it's slipcovered in white fabric. Try
this easy-to-clean, kid-friendly solution
whether you live in the city or the country.

FLOAT YOUR SHELVES

There's no such thing as dead space.
Create vertical storage in an otherwise
empty corner by installing a series of
floating shelves, then pop in a chair so
you'll have a place to sit back and listen
to music or read a book.

TRY A CLEAR COFFEE TABLE

A glass top almost becomes invisible in a room—and makes the distance between a sofa and chairs appear greater. Another added bonus: You can view more of a beautiful print rug underneath. In a small space, consider a Moroccan-style pouf as a footrest or for extra seating.

USE A SIDEBOARD

Often referred to as a credenza or buffet, and traditionally used in a dining room to conceal dishes and serving pieces, this long and low cabinet is perfect for living spaces, too. Use the top for display and fill the interior with your less artful (but more functional!) belongings.

DISGUISE YOUR TECH

Camouflage your big black box by making it blend in with your décor. In this space, the homeowner stacked two reclaimed paint shelves to create an entertainment unit that houses books, treasures, and, yes, a TV (that you barely see!).

USE FURNITURE TO CREATE "ROOMS"

Maximize your living space by rearranging the furniture. Placing a console table behind the chairs divides the room. The main space is great for watching TV, while the nook in the back is a comfy spot to sit and enjoy the great river view. Use different coffee tables, furniture styles, and even rugs to help make areas feel distinct.

FRAME THE FIREPLACE

Install wood panels to give your fireplace a dramatic redo. The key to keeping it cost-effective: Don't change the original firebox or remove old brick—just cover them up! Add built-in storage on either side. Place the TV above the mantel and keep all the electrical wires behind the wood panels. Use a magazine rack for firewood and papers.

HOW TO STYLE SHELVES

Creating displays on open shelving is as much of an art as it is an organizing solution. Here's how the pros do it.

1 START WITH BOOKS. Whether you stack them vertically or horizontally, all shelves need books. Large, hardcover options will look impressive, so place them on lower shelves. Reserve upper shelves for smaller paperbacks. For both, try to group by color.

2 ADD ART AND COLLECTIBLES. Pull together unique and treasured pieces from your travels. Think small statues, ceramic vases, or other curios you've collected along the way. Give more breathing space to larger objects, so they stand out. Use small ones to finish off a stack of books.

3 LAYER IN TRAYS AND BASKETS. Here's your chance to gain more storage for your less pretty things and also bring in a variety of different shapes, textures, and materials. Glass or metal trays, plus woven baskets, complement any home decorating style.

SECRETS TO A CLUTTER-FREE ENTERTAINMENT CENTER

Get your living room company-ready with these tricks and tools.

STASH ACCESSORIES OUT OF SIGHT

Entertainment rooms may have two to three remotes that can take up valuable space on a coffee table and often go missing. Designate a drawer or bin for these items—and make it a rule to return them to that spot when you turn off the TV. If you have a collection of DVDs, sort them by genre (rom-coms, kids') and store them in dustproof paperboard boxes.

CUT CORD CLUTTER

Get the shortest cord you need for the job. Label both ends of cables with colored tape so it's easy to know which goes where. Use ties to keep the cords together and unjumbled, and secure any excess with a twist tie.

KEEP DUST AT BAY

Regularly wipe down the TV screen with a dry microfiber cloth; cleansers may harm its coating. De-fuzz speakers using the soft-brush attachment of your vacuum cleaner; bristles get into crevices without scratching the finish. Catch dust bunnies under heavy pieces with a flexible dust-grabber.

SANITIZE REMOTES

As one of the most fought-over and often-touched gadgets in your home, remotes can be as bacteria-laden as toilet handles! Carefully de-gunk the buttons with a toothpick, and then swab the remote all over with a disinfecting wipe.

1-MINUTE TIP! **Pile high.** Instantly spruce up the surface of a coffee table or side table by organizing books in neat stacks. Start with the largest books on the bottom and align spines so they face out. Place small curios on top of each stack for a decorative touch.

SMARTER SIDE TABLES

More than just a place to drop the TV remote, these living room essentials can provide sneaky storage when you think outside the box.

USE DRESSERS

Why banish these great storage solutions to the bedroom? Two compact chests with drawers provide ample hidden storage space in a living room, too! Look for ones with three drawers and use them for all the accessories that are best kept out of sight.

BE FLEXIBLE

It's worth it to keep a pair of light and airy ottomans in your living room. Flexible furnishings like this can be easily moved around to function as extra seating when needed or as a spot to place drinks. Choose ones in a neutral shade and timeless style so they can also be moved from room to room.

TRY TWO SHELVES

A second shelf instantly doubles the storage potential of a side table. Use the top shelf for a table lamp and decorative elements like fresh-cut flowers or a ceramic figurine. Place a box on the lower shelf to corral remotes, playing cards, or game pieces, or use it to neatly stack books and magazines.

OPT FOR A GIANT BASKET

If you have tons of stuff to put away every day, like children's or pet toys, but also need to access them often, consider a large, deep, circular basket in place of a side table. You can toss things inside in a matter of seconds for an instantly organized space.

BRING IN A BAR CART

This handy household piece is making a comeback—and we couldn't be more thrilled. Place it beside the couch and you'll get more storage than a traditional side or end table, as well as the additional benefit of easy access to your wine collection when entertaining. To add an extra layer of convenience, look for one that comes with wheels!

HUTCH HELP

It could be a flea-market find or brand-new, but a glass-front hutch is a great way to maximize storage in the living room. Place it beside the couch or side chair and fill it with well-loved pieces, like pottery, vases, and more. Take advantage of the space below to sneak in a large basket for extra blankets.

POWER OF THREE

A trio of nesting tables can be pulled out
to create more surface space when you're
entertaining. Then they tuck neatly away
when not in use. Decorate the top with
simple elements, like fresh-cut flowers
and a small tray.

PERFECT CATCHALL

Some side tables, like this modern copper one, are more decorative than functional for storage. In that case, simply place a slim wire basket in front of it. Use the basket to keep your collection of books and magazines.

READING NOOK

A gallery wall of framed black-and-white photographs is the perfect opportunity to showcase beautiful artwork in a chic and streamlined way—and offer a clever distraction from the TV. A trio of étagères provide chic storage for books and more.

HOW TO ORGANIZE A GALLERY WALL

It just takes a little time (and patience!) to mark where you want everything placed, but once you nail that, the rest is a piece of cake.

1 GATHER YOUR ART AND PHOTOS. Grab what you plan to put up and play around with the grouping until you find the best arrangement. Then snap a photo with your phone.

2 TRACE EACH FRAME. Outline them on pieces of paper and cut them out. (Tip: Try a roll of kraft paper for pieces larger than 8 × 10 inches.)

3 REVIEW YOUR GROUPING. Refer to your photo to temporarily adhere the paper cutouts to the wall, using a level and painter's tape.

4 MEASURE THE DISTANCE. Check the amount of space between the top of the actual frame and where the center of the nail needs to go, then mark this distance on each of the hanging paper cutouts.

5 GRAB YOUR HAMMER. Nail right through the paper cutouts into the wall, on your marks. Rip away the paper, hang up your frames, then step back and admire your masterpiece.

MIRROR IMAGE

Forget about pushing the back of a
worktable up against a wall. Instead,
get double the space by placing the
shorter side adjacent to the wall, or in a
convenient spot in the room, and adding
one workstation on each side. Use the
same accessories for both to achieve a
streamlined look.

WORK + CRAFT SPACES

Make the most of your home office or craft space by creating a zone that actually motivates you to get the job done! A sense of orderliness here ensures that you'll be more productive and efficient, and less distracted by clutter. Whether it's an entire room or a craft corner, banish mess with dozens of great ideas for easy filing, desk-clearing office essentials, and the best ways to manage tech.

PRO ORGANIZER TIPS TO STEAL

There are loads of sneaky ways to carve out a neat and tidy home office, whether you have a dedicated room or not. Here are some of our favorite tricks.

TRICK OUT A TABLE

Give a workstation a lift by attaching caster wheels to the bottom. The result? A mobile office that moves around as your work—and your space—call for it. In this mudroom-meets-office, hooks, shelves, and metal storage bins offer loads of flexibility.

MAXIMIZE SHELVES

Build out a wall of open shelving for a
pretty and practical organizing solution.
Select a mix of containers and vertical
sorters in neutral colors so the entire
zone feels cohesive from floor to ceiling.
Pepper in a few decorative pieces in
complementary shades to amp up the style.

CONVERT A CLOSET

Reconfigure a rarely used pantry or closet—whether it's in a kitchen, basement, or bedroom—into a mini-office. Pile it high with plenty of shallow shelving to create a productive place to check off your to-do list. Instead of installing a bulky desk, place one of the shelves at desk height and use it as a desk. Add a magnetic board on the wall to keep inspirational photos and supplies.

TURN A NOOK INTO
A WORKSPACE

A desk and a task lamp transform an
unused alcove—in any room—into the
perfect place for projects. Pair it with a
slim chair that easily tucks in to ensure
that the "office" uses the least amount
of space possible.

MAKE OVER AN ARMOIRE

Retrofit a dated piece of furniture into a
compact yet highly functional mini-office.
Attach letter holders and clipboards to the
inside of the doors, then coat them with
chalkboard paint to give kids and adults
alike a place to jot down reminders or
make notes.

Disguise tech as art.

GET COMPACT

A light and airy powder-blue desk with slim legs and barely there hardware fits easily into almost any room—and it's a great way to disguise a large heating vent. Install a tiny floating shelf on the wall above to mix a few pieces of artwork in with your digital devices.

HANDY HUTCH

Ditch the traditional desk setup for this savvy space-saving idea. Install a brightly painted floating hutch on a spare wall for a "desk" that's there when you need it and hidden when you don't. Ingenious!

SET UP UNDER THE STAIRS

Tuck a fully stocked office beside or (even better!) under a staircase. A rich wooden desk with built-in storage drawers and powder-coated steel rails, combined with a studded leather chair, add modern edge against a white wall. Lean a chalkboard against the wall to reduce the need for paper notes.

Decorative boxes add style and storage.

HOW TO DECLUTTER YOUR DESK IN SECONDS

Buried in bills, receipts, and papers? Never have enough room to work?
Try these tricks to banish the mess in no time.

1 MAXIMIZE YOUR SPACE. Mount a shelf (or two!) above the area to keep frequently used supplies and tools handy, but off your desk. Place a large bin on the floor to collect trash. Use decorative storage boxes or trays to keep documents in order.

2 GET A DAILY PLANNER. Whether you choose a traditional paper planner or a smartphone app, having a portable place to keep your notes and contacts, plus your calendar and list of tasks, will make it easier to find what you need and prioritize.

3 DESIGNATE A TO-DO BIN. Avoid the out-of-sight, out-of-mind trap. Place papers that need priority attention in a drawer or a special spot near your entryway. They'll be harder to ignore when you pass them every day.

4 CREATE A RECEIPT DROP ZONE. Tuck all sales slips into a folder and leave it in an obvious spot. When it's full, sort through for essential receipts, then stow them in your filing cabinet. Ditch backlogs of bank statements, bills, and pay stubs—most need to be kept for only a year.

5 LIGHT IT RIGHT. If you often work at night or don't have a good natural light source nearby, make sure your workstation has proper task lighting. An adjustable-height desk lamp will help you keep your focus on the task at hand.

6 GET A PROPER FILING CABINET. Whether you choose a portable solution or invest in a larger unit, it's helpful to have a single spot to stash important papers, like insurance policies, birth certificates, and health records. Opt for a cabinet on wheels, which can be tucked away when it's not in use and also doubles as a surface extender, when needed.

7 GET HELP WITH BILLS AND FINANCES. Use tools like the app **Expensify** to make it simpler to budget and track your finances. Digitize receipts so you can search for them easily and have less clutter.

8 BE SMART WITH PASSWORDS. Don't use the same passwords for everything. Keep your passwords safe, secure, and easily accessible with a digital app like **Dashlane** or **LastPass**, which creates secure passwords and checks the security levels of your current ones. Plus, the password app can autofill info in apps and web pages.

HIDE STUFF IN DECORATIVE BOXES

Stylish stackable containers are great for organizing potential eyesores, like manuals, extra printer paper, or ink cartridges. Choose boxes with built-in labels so you always know what's inside.

CORRAL SUPPLIES ON A TRAY

If your desk has few or no drawers, group necessary tools and accessories together on a tray that you can simply move aside when you need room to spread out. Use a pretty glass or tray for pencils and a second smaller one for loose paper or binder clips.

MAKE YOUR OWN COMMAND CENTRAL

Install a giant bulletin board near your workstation to create a practical statement wall that gives loose papers, calendars, and important files a place to land.

USE CORK SHEETS

Attach cork sheets from a hardware store or an office-supply store to your wall with nails or thumbtacks.

CREATE ZONES WITH COLOR

If neutral cork isn't your style, use a small roller to paint on blocks of color and designate each as its own to-do "zone."

CLIP IT UP

Craft a rotating display of important memos and notes by nailing pretty clipboards (available at Staples®) to the wall and using them to keep papers in sight.

STICK IT ON WITH MAGNETS

Steal this spice rack trick to corral paper clips, tacks, and more in jars attached to metal strips. Just add adhesive magnets to their bases and stick 'em up.

LABEL WITH STYLE

Use colorful washi tape and a fine-tip permanent marker to label cords, making it a cinch to figure out what's plugged in behind the TV or on a power strip.

ESSENTIAL FILING QUESTIONS

1 DO YOU HAVE A SYSTEM?

One of the best filing methods is a simple alphabetical system, organized by the first letter of the topic. Keep filed papers in order, so any single file is organized from newest in front to oldest in back, or vice versa.

2 DO YOU HAVE ENOUGH SPACE?

If you are cramming files into an overstuffed cabinet, you may be tempted to throw away essential papers, and you will have trouble accessing the ones you need. Be realistic about your file-storage space and add another cabinet, if needed.

3 CAN IT GO DIGITAL?

A lot of what was once retained and stored as paper can be converted to digital files. You can file taxes and see bank statements online; copies of correspondence can be kept on your hard drive or saved to the cloud. And now product information is often available on companies' websites or as software supplied with electronic products. So you don't need to keep the paper versions (recycle them!).

TRICKS FOR DEALING WITH PAPER OVERLOAD

Learn how to dig out with these strategies.

GO DIGITAL

Consider switching to paperless billing—it's a great way to cut back on paper clutter. Then automate payments. If you're not ready to go 100-percent paperless, scan bills, download to your computer, and then shred the hard copies. If you're attached to paying by check, stash your checkbook, stamps, return-address stickers, and unpaid invoices in one place, like a portable mesh bin.

SHRED IT

Pass on a shredder that clips onto a trash can, even though it saves space—you have to take it out, put it on, and plug it in. Instead, choose a binned shredder that crosscuts (to protect your privacy) and has a higher sheet capacity than you may need, say, 10 sheets at a time. The single smartest thing you can do to protect against identity theft is to invest in a crosscut shredder, like **Fellowes® Powershred® M-8C**. We love it because it takes on 8 sheets at a time and copes with paper clips, credit cards, and staples.

PUT YOUR MAILBOX ON A DIET

Go to dmachoice.org and optoutprescreen.com to remove your name from mailing lists. Call card issuers and ask them to stop sending stuff like balance transfer checks (you can request them later if needed). When shopping online, uncheck boxes letting brands mail you catalogs or promos.

PRINT ON BOTH SIDES

Cut down on paper waste by using both sides of every sheet. On one side, write or print drafts of school essays, driving directions, etc. Then flip the page over for a brand-new sheet. Store new and used pages in separate bins so you can grab either easily.

STOP THE (PRINTING) PRESSES

Make PDFs of online purchase confirmation pages and save them in a folder called RECEIPTS until your shipment arrives. On both PCs and Macs, select the Print to PDF or the Print to File option. On Macs, you can also export to PDF.

3 WAYS TO PROTECT IMPORTANT PAPERS

1 CONTAIN. Organize tax returns (the IRS can audit you up to six years back) and other long-term keepers by year in sturdy expandable folders inside plastic bins. They'll be out of sight but safe, even in a dusty attic or a leaky basement.

2 FILE. Stash papers you'd otherwise stack willy-nilly around the house in a lockable filing cabinet. Label hanging file folders with names like FAMILY, TAXES, MEDICAL, AUTO, LEGAL, HOME, SCHOOL, WORK, and MISCELLANEOUS (subdivide them more, if you like). Then take the in-and-out approach: When a new policy goes in, the old one comes out.

3 PROTECT. Get a fire- and waterproof box. And make sure it locks! Fill it with difficult-to-replace documents (birth certificates and marriage licenses, passports, Social Security cards, wills, copies of prescriptions). Also, include a list of accounts (banking, investment, credit card), emergency contacts (doctors, next of kin), and an inventory of household valuables. Scan all these documents and back them up on a hard drive.

4 WAYS TO KEEP TRACK OF OLD PHOTOS

Here's how to keep the memories alive—without the clutter.

1 BE RUTHLESS. Collect photos in one place, and then do a serious sorting-out job, ditching all but the best. Store them in top-quality boxes and albums. What's essential: acid-free paper, which keeps images from deteriorating. Storage bins should also be acid-free—so, no shoeboxes.

2 BOX BY YEAR. The easiest way to organize is in chronological order, so sort prints and disks into boxes by year and, within that, by season; then label. Mark envelopes with colored-dot stickers for specific categories (e.g., school events: blue; holidays: green; etc.).

3 HOLD ON TO ANY NEGATIVES. Don't let the digital revolution fool you: Negatives are still never to be trashed, lest you lose prints or want to make new copies later. Clip negatives, separated by subject, and stash them in envelopes with their print counterparts.

4 TAKE ADVANTAGE OF DIGITAL SERVICES. Store digital pics at an online photo site (we like **snapfish.com**). For a small fee—or for free—you get low-cost prints plus online album space. This also helps prevent computer clutter. You can also use a service like **Memories Renewed** or Google's **PhotoScan** app.

HOW TO ORGANIZE DIGITAL FILES

Don't let your computer become the dumping ground your desk used to be.

Throwing everything into one big MY DOCUMENTS folder—or, worse, onto your desktop—makes it difficult to find files and can slow down your machine. Create a structure of folders and subfolders that makes sense for your home and business needs so you can find and file things fast. Force frequently used folders to the top of an alphabetical list by naming them with a symbol, like a plus sign (+), as the first character.

5 CUTE WAYS TO SHOW OFF YOUR PICS

Stop grabbing your phone to see vacation or graduation photos. Display them 24/7 with the help of these services.

1 CREATE A CALENDAR.
Artifact Uprising allows you to design your own easy-to-hang clipboard calendar, with everything from cards and calendars to framed wall art and personalized books. Pick a collection of pics or import photos from social media.

2 MAKE MAGNETS.
Print Studio turns social media snaps into cool gifts, like photo-booth-style prints, right from your phone. Download the app and choose your favorite photos.

3 HANG A METAL PHOTO.
WhiteWall is a go-to source for printing images on unexpected surfaces. Prints on metal aren't likely to fade or warp—ideal for humid or outdoor spaces.

4 CRAFT A COLLAGE.
Minted makes your walls shine with its photo art. Add your shots to predesigned templates, like the ultra-personalized collages—and that's it! Thanks to silver, gold, or rose-gold foil and loads of frame options, each creation is truly one-of-a-kind.

5 COMPILE A BOOK.
Pinhole Press turns family snaps into educational toys, like photo books, puzzles, and games. Board books are great for helping little ones learn names and faces and the thick card stock stands up to sticky fingers.

BOOST PHOTO SMARTS

Apple users, grab your devices and check your settings. Here's the lowdown on two features you need to know about.

iCLOUD PHOTO LIBRARY

This setting syncs photos among all your devices (iOS 8.3 and up)—so when you take a picture on your iPhone, it's instantly uploaded to the cloud and shared with your iPad and MacBook (via Wi-Fi). **TOP TIP:** Be careful— now when you delete an image from one place, it's deleted everywhere. Trash something by mistake? Look for the RECENTLY DELETED folder, where videos and pics are saved for 30 days.

OPTIMIZE IPHONE STORAGE

Turn on this setting to keep lower-resolution photos and videos (which take up less space) on your phone while high-quality ones stay in the cloud. Just click on a photo or video when you want to view, edit, or share it, and the higher-res version appears.

END GADGET MAYHEM

8 brilliant steps to controlling office tech and cord chaos.

1 CREATE A CHARGING ZONE.
Park frequently used gadgets at a multislotted charging station, which will keep items juiced and orderly. Match labels on cords to those in the gadget slots. Corral cords with easy-to-fasten-and-unfasten Velcro wraps; this trick can work wonders in your computer and TV zones, too. Plug devices into a surge protector, opting for a version you can switch off to conserve electricity.

2 KEEP IMPORTANT PAPERWORK.
Hold on to receipts, manuals, and warranty info for the life of your devices. Try to hang on to packaging, too, for the initial warranty periods or however long the store accepts returns; then move paperwork into a binder sleeve labeled with device names and purchase dates. Also, register products online to stay abreast of updates.

3 DON'T LOSE ANYTHING. Thirty percent of people don't back up files, and every three seconds someone's hard drive fails. You could get an external drive, or rely on the cloud—backup on a website that uses multiple servers so your data will be safe in case of crashes. Set up an account on a site like sugarsync.com or dropbox.com for a low monthly fee.

4 REBOOT YOUR BATTERIES.
Use rechargeable batteries, rather than stocking regular AAs. You'll have less to store, and you'll be saving money and hassle as well as helping out the environment.

5 DITCH OLD DEVICES. Toss nonworking or unwanted electronics, but do so wisely, as they can leak mercury and lead into the soil or groundwater. Use in-store take-back programs, which often offer incentives for returns; check your town for local electronics recycling programs; or look up area e-cyclers on **earth911.com**. Don't forget to get rid of the cords and other attachments to lessen confusion (and clutter) later.

6 MOVE FILES OFF YOUR DESKTOP.
Clutter on a computer desktop actually slows down performance. Don't save unneeded files there. Take a second to put them into a hard-drive folder; a basic MY PHOTOS or MY DOCUMENTS label is fine.

7 KEEP SCREENS CLEAN. Stow microfiber cloths and screen-cleaning spray in a drawer, basket, or bin near your charging station so you can spruce up items as you take them out. Stash an extra microfiber cloth in your device's carrying case (or a purse pocket) for on-the-go cleaning. Peripheral pieces like cords, connectors, USB drives, and converters will stay untangled yet visible in zippered mesh pouches.

8 CHECK YOUR BACKUP. No gadget is an island. Back up music, photos, and cell numbers on a phone SIM card, your home computer, an external hard drive, or the cloud. That way, you'll be protected even if your device fails.

DE-GUNK YOUR MOST-USED GADGETS

BUST DUST ON KEYBOARDS.

Use a can of compressed air or a soft, clean brush to whisk away dirt that causes keys to stick and trackballs to stop rolling. If that's not enough, grab a premoistened electronics cleaning wipe (wring out excess moisture) and, with a toothpick, work it into the crevices around the buttons and the ball. If home remedies don't work, take the device in for service.

CLEAN OUT YOUR EAR(BUD)S.

Don't be surprised your earphones' sound quality is suffering if the last time you cleaned them was never. To remove grime, gently go over the buds with a small brush. If the covers or caps are removable, pop them off and soak for about 30 minutes in hot water mixed with dishwashing liquid. Rinse and dry. For one-piece earphones, dip the tip of a cotton swab in rubbing alcohol, squeeze out excess, and go over all sides. Use the swab's other end to wipe and dry.

STORE & DISPLAY

Try keeping ribbons on spools to make them easy to pull out and cut. Repurpose mason jars to keep things like buttons or gift accessories in view, but out of reach of young children.

CRAFTY IDEA

Some items are too lovely to keep hidden away in a drawer. Create an artful display with pretty supplies, like colorful rolls of wrapping paper, for an organizing solution that doubles as eye-catching wall art.

SEE CLEARLY

Group supplies by purpose, sorting
by color, season, or brand—whichever
best suits your work style. Then stash
materials in labeled see-through
containers so finding them is extra easy.
Keep frequently used items—scissors,
glue, paper—within easy reach.

MAXIMIZE YOUR CRAFT ZONE

Those super-organized crafting rooms you see online? You can have one, too.

PLAN YOUR SETUP

If you have a dedicated craft area, pick storage that keeps your work surface clear but supplies within reach, such as wall shelves for bins and baskets or a hanging rod for hooks and cups. Get a portable organizer, like a tackle box or a toolbox, for smaller supplies and tools. Protect work surfaces with nonstick oilcloth (it's your DIY splat mat), plug in an adjustable task light, and you're ready for inspiration to strike.

ORGANIZE SUPPLIES

Let's be honest: Crayon boxes rip way too easily. Instead, store coloring items in a plastic desk organizer and devote each drawer to a different collection. Launching a big project? Gather materials in color-coded, labeled boxes, so must-haves will be on hand when you need them. "File" tricky-to-store items like paint pouches, sticker packs, and paper punches in open bins.

ROLL WITH IT

If you only have a craft nook, not a whole room, invest in a cart on wheels that goes anywhere and keeps your materials organized. Select one with semitransparent drawers that let you identify the contents easily. Presort scrapbooking embellishments by season, occasion, or hue so they're easy to locate.

SEW SMART

Slip embroidery floss into zip-top bags, separated by color or number (if you work from patterns). Place folded fabrics vertically in bins, rather than laying them flat, for better viewing of—and access to—the prints and colors at your disposal.

THINK DOUBLE-DUTY

Snag storage solutions from all around the house. Small food jars can be affixed to the undersides of shelves to hold baubles without causing clutter: Screw lids from salvaged jars to shelves, then twist jars on. Raid your closet for a skirt hanger and use it to clip oversize scrapbooking papers. If you're working in a guest room or home office, closet-rod shelving and over-the-door shoe bags hold supplies out of sight when company comes.

STREAMLINE REGULARLY

KEEP

1 Food packaging for clever storage: Styrofoam or cardboard produce trays are perfect for corralling in-process projects, while lidded jars, tins, and boxes can hold trinkets—for free.

2 Silica gel packets from shoe boxes: Slip them into your fabric stash to minimize humidity. Avoid keeping supplies in a basement or garage where the temperature fluctuates.

3 An extension cord handy: This way your electric tools (hot-glue gun, hobby drill) are always able to reach the power.

TOSS

Old supplies: Pitch dried-out paints or glues, crinkled papers, faded fabrics, and other damaged supplies yearly. Donate any unused supplies in good condition to a child-care center, retirement home, community arts council, or crafty friend.

SUPERB SYMMETRY

Two of everything—from the table lamps and nightstands to the accent chairs and throw pillows—helps create a balanced room. This trick is a great way to pull off a cohesive, instantly ordered look.

BEDROOMS

Find your escape from the day's stresses with a bedroom-turned-retreat, thanks to a few of our mess-busting tips and tricks. Tackle tough spots—we're talking about you, cluttered bedside table and overflowing drawers!—and up your storage space by giving life to underutilized nooks and crannies.

PRO ORGANIZER TIPS TO STEAL

Make sure your sleep zone is a peaceful haven by following these tricks to eliminate clutter.

UPGRADE THE NIGHTSTAND

Replace your traditional bedside table, which typically offers very little storage, with a large dresser. Look for a chest with two to three drawers that has a similar footprint to a nightstand but offers more height.

PAINT THE CEILING

When you coat your walls in a soothing hue, like Harbor Haze from Benjamin Moore Natura® (shown here), consider extending the color onto the ceiling to reduce visual clutter. A soft, creamy shade for the mantel and bed linens, and soft-patterned curtains, complete the cozy, sophisticated vibe.

ADD A BENCH

Take advantage of the empty space at the foot of the bed to put a bench or a pair of ottomans with added storage.

HANG BEDSIDE LAMPS

When you're short on nightstand real estate, regain valuable surface space by swapping in a slim, wall-mounted sconce instead of a table lamp. Choose one with a swinging arm for easier nighttime reading.

USE BASKETS AND TRAYS

Strategically placed wicker baskets help corral and contain clutter. Decorative trays in various sizes are perfect for making things that could look haphazard and messy—like candles with matches, coins from your pocket, or a few pieces of jewelry—look pulled together instead.

Line up photos above the bed.

PUT UP A SLIM SHELF

Install a floating shelf above the headboard to show off a collection of family photos. Choose color or black-and-white photographs. Feel free to vary the size of the frames, but keep in mind that it will look more organized if they all match in size and color.

Dress the bed with graphic textiles.

DREAMY HEADBOARD

Make over a basic bed frame with this cheap space-saving trick: Use painter's tape and a level to mark a rectangle on the wall, apply two coats of paint, then peel the tape away. Sweet dreams!

8 INGENIOUS WAYS TO MASTER BEDROOM MESS

Whether you have five minutes or an hour, a few simple fixes can transform your sleeping space into an organized (and relaxing!) getaway.

1 GIVE YOUR NIGHTSTAND A CLEAN SWEEP. End the day with a calming bedside view. Empty the drawer and put back only what you use nightly or weekly (e.g., hand cream, an eye mask). Cull finished magazines—give them to a local library or senior center—and implement a six-books-max rule: No more on display!

2 CLEAN OFF THE CHAIR. Don't let a pretty seat become a laundry drop zone. Either leave washed items in the dryer until you have time to fold them or tuck them in a lidded basket by your dresser.

3 CLEAR THE FLOOR OF FOOTWEAR. Brown wicker baskets snuggled into a savvy bed frame are perfect for storing shoes and slippers. Plus, a cozy white blanket could almost conceal this storage spot entirely.

4 DECLUTTER THE TOP OF YOUR DRESSER. Embrace your habits when it comes to this dumping ground. Empty your pockets? Add a cup for coins and a wastebasket for tissues and receipts. Read the mail? A letter sorter will keep bills up front. Try on jewelry? Use a clear bowl to prevent chunky pieces from piling up.

5 HANG UP BAGS. Stop dropping your tote on your bed or (worse) the floor. Hooks on the inside of your closet door will offer space for your entire collection. Plus, it makes picking out a purse that matches your outfit so much easier.

6 SPIFF UP YOUR LINGERIE DRAWER. Get rid of frayed underwear, stretched-out items (even if you love the color), and anything uncomfortable. Use thin cardboard to sort what's left: Hot-glue strips together to create cubbies or insert cut-down tissue boxes as sock and undies compartments.

7 STASH UNSIGHTLY CHARGERS. Make your phone charger look like it's just part of your bedtime reading routine by creating a hollow space in a patterned notebook (once you've used up all the pages). It'll make your nightstand look neat and pretty.

8 DITCH ANYTHING WORK-RELATED. Not only do prime offenders, like your laptop, tablet, and paperwork, clutter up your space and collect hard-to-remove dust, they can also be distracting. Relocate them to another spot in the house for more space—and peace of mind.

MAKE SHEETS STAND OUT

Dress the bed with a colorful set (like bold citron—pow!), then fold the top over, hotel-style, to make sure the bedding gets the attention it deserves. Add a punchy graphic blanket at the foot of the bed for contrast.

8 SECRETS TO A SLEEK GUEST ROOM

Company's coming! Make visitors feel right at home with these ultra-quick organizing and spruce-up secrets.

1 CLEAR OUT EXTRA STUFF. Declutter the area where guests will sleep, whether it's a guest room or the living room. Stash things in lidded boxes or bins, which can be left out or tucked away. The goal: Give visitors space for their shoes, jewelry, and more. Instead of emptying drawers, get a few inexpensive luggage racks.

2 TEST-DRIVE THE SPACE. Before they arrive, hang out (or actually snooze) in their soon-to-be sleeping area to see what is and isn't working. (Lamp needs a new bulb? Cobwebs in the ceiling corners? TV remote needs batteries?) And don't forget clean sheets, blankets, pillows, and an alarm clock. For extra points, leave a bedside water carafe.

3 INSTALL EASY-ACCESS HOOKS. Don't want anyone to see what's lurking inside your closet? Save your dump-it-all zone from scrutiny and give guests a place to hang clothes with an over-the-door hook stocked with hangers.

4 DRESS THE BED FOR SLEEP AND STYLE. Pop pillows into the dryer on the no-heat setting for 10 minutes to fluff them and remove any dust. Offer up a lighter blanket with your winter comforter to give guests options. As you make up the bed with clean linens, spritz the fitted sheet with linen spray.

5 MOVE BREAKABLES. Take away anything fragile, expensive, or sentimental from common areas or guest rooms. It'll lower your stress level (and theirs!), especially if they're traveling with kids.

6 PLACE IMPORTANT INFO IN SIGHT. Keep brochures for local attractions, maps, and transit schedules in a folder for out-of-towners. Also include a list of your home's must-knows (like the address, cross streets, and alarm code) and current local event listings. Spare house keys, color-coded and stored on a clip, are always helpful.

7 START A MINI–LENDING LIBRARY. Hosting a bookworm? Leave a few titles you've already read by the bed and let your guest know it's okay to finish them back at home.

8 MAKE SOME CLOSET SPACE. If you're okay with letting them peek inside, free up space for guests' clothes by removing 10 items or so currently hanging in the closet. Replace with empty hangers for guests to use. Empty the contents of the top dresser drawer into a box and slip the box under the bed. Set a pretty dish on the nightstand to hold jewelry and loose change.

3 SNEAKY WAYS TO GAIN MORE STORAGE

Try these clever strategies to boost storage without sacrificing serenity.

1 **USE THE BACKS OF DOORS.** Fight the temptation to throw things on a chair or bench by affixing or hanging hooks to the back of your bedroom and closet doors. If you choose the kind that hook over the door, you won't have to worry about damage caused by drilling holes, using screws, or sticking on adhesive. This is also the perfect place for a pocketed shoe organizer.

---

2 **GO UNDER.** If your closet is at maximum capacity, consider under-the-bed storage units. Most hold a dozen pairs of shoes or more, and ones on wheels are super-easy to roll in and out. Grab a few and dedicate each one to heels, sandals, or flats. Or use this space to keep off-season clothing or extra bed linens hidden but within easy reach. Try the same strategy under your nightstand or chair. Just make sure to choose the appropriate style. If the containers are visible, you want them to be pretty. But if they're camouflaged by a bed skirt, hard plastic is fine.

3 **UPSIZE YOUR DRESSER.** Why settle for the standard four-drawer unit? If you have the wall space, opt for a taller five- or six-drawer dresser. It will take up the same amount of floor space, but give you 25–50 percent more vertical storage, depending on the height of the drawers. Just think of all the things you could hide there!

BUILD A BETTER BEDSIDE TABLE

Try these tricks to make this essential bedroom piece work overtime.

BE SMART ABOUT LIGHTING

Consider wall sconces, which will free up surface space and allow you to control what you illuminate. Or use a lamp with a small footprint to take up the least amount of surface space as possible.

MAKE A PLACE FOR CHANGE

Every bedside tabletop needs a holder for loose change, keys, rings, and anything else you need to retrieve quickly. It can be as simple as a cup, bowl, woven basket, or something more decorative, like a tiered serving dish or wooden tray. Whatever you choose, a valet will keep pocket-size items in one place.

DON'T FORGET THE WALL

If you aren't mounting lights, that doesn't mean you should leave the walls empty. Use the space to hang a mirror, tiny shelves for books or a potted plant, or even simple hooks, which could hold jewelry or other accessories you want to take off at night and put on again in the morning.

TRICKS FOR PERFECTLY ORDERED DRAWERS

INVEST IN DIVIDERS.

Spring-loaded, flexible inserts transform a cluttered underwear drawer into a streamlined system that's as beautiful as it is functional. Start by editing out tattered, ill-fitting, or uncomfortable items. Group undies by type (brief, bikini, etc.). For bras, fold one cup into the other so cups keep their shape and take up less space.

"FILE" YOUR T-SHIRTS.

Instead of piling T-shirts on top of one another, fold them a bit smaller and "file" them from front to back with the folded edges facing up. You'll find what you need at a glance, and when you pull one out, the others will remain neatly in place.

ROLL IT.

Slippery garments like pajamas, silk lingerie, scarves, and camisoles get messy in a hurry when folded and stacked in a drawer. Instead, tuck pajama tops into bottoms and roll them together. Line up all the rolls so you can easily find what you're looking for.

HANG SWEATERS.

Yes, you can hang sweaters if drawer space is tight. But don't hang them as you would a blouse. Instead, fold them in half vertically, matching up the sleeves, then place the hook of the hanger at the armpit. Fold the sleeves over one side and the body over the other. This keeps the sweater from stretching and prevents those little shoulder bumps.

MIRROR MAGIC

Instead of placing a dressing mirror on the back of the door or using up other valuable wall real estate, consider leaning it above an empty nightstand. Just make sure the table is sturdy enough to handle the extra weight!

TURN PIECES INTO ART

Keep jewelry from junking up your
dresser by stowing your most-worn pieces
in shadow boxes near your dressing area.
Mount artwork or a photo behind the glass
and use pushpins to hold things in place.
Or put up pieces of painted corkboard
and drape your favorite necklaces and
bracelets over the pushpins.

7 SMART WAYS TO STORE JEWELRY

Accessories are fun, but they can end up scattered all over.
Here's how to restore order and quickly find what you need.

1 USE A TRAY . . . OR A BOWL. Place everyday items in a cute bowl or on a small tray. To keep pieces from getting tangled, hang earrings around the edge of the bowl and place rings in the center. Or hang necklaces and bracelets on a metal jewelry tree.

2 SORT SCARVES FOR EASY ACCESS. Hang them by type, color, and occasion to find the perfect one in seconds, whether you're hitting the slopes or heading for Sunday brunch. Or place a few in a glass bowl that lives on a shelf. You're more likely to accessorize with a scarf if you see it out.

3 GIVE A TRAVEL POUCH A TRY. Soft jewelry cases and rolls are attractive enough to place on top of your dresser but can easily be stored in a drawer as well. The soft lining keeps special pieces from getting scratched.

4 REPURPOSE OTHER ITEMS. Instead of taking empty shoeboxes and paper towel rolls to the curb, cover them in a feminine fabric or scrapbooking paper to create a delicate watch and bangle holder. Try a candlestick to stack bracelets, or a cutlery divider to separate necklaces and brooches.

5 BUTTON UP YOUR EARRINGS. If you're always misplacing one earring or its back, hook pairs through the holes of a spare button. They'll be easier to find and look cute in your jewelry box. An ice cube tray is also an inexpensive way to store pairs. Keep mateless earrings or broken baubles in their own container so it's easy to find them at repair (or reunion) time.

6 GET SOME STACKABLE DIVIDED TRAYS. Velvet-lined ones let you store and protect necklaces, rings, bracelets, and more while being able to see what you have at a glance. They come in a wide variety of configurations and can be stacked inside a drawer so they don't clutter the dresser top. In a pinch, even a plastic ice cube tray can work for small items like rings, earrings, and pins.

7 HIDE THEM INSIDE A CLOSET. Jewelry organizers with small pouches that can be hung from a closet rod or a hook on the back of a door are slim and easy to store and use. Most can accommodate long and short pieces and will keep your items displayed so finding what you want quickly will be a cinch.

JOY MANGANO BETTER BEAUTY CASES

These useful bags, available in three sizes and an array of colors, unroll to reveal individual removable zippered plastic pouches for the ultimate in organization—whether you're storing makeup, jewelry, craft supplies, or other small items.

MIX IT UP

Outfit your closet area with a combination
of full- and half-height hanging racks,
drawers, and shelves for added storage
up top (perfect for off-season gear).
A set of pull-out hampers can help keep
laundry in order.

HOW TO TACKLE CLOTHES CLOSET CLUTTER

Make room for everything—plus, find extra space even if you only have 20 minutes.

DOUBLE UP ON HANGERS

Who knew those metal tabs that come on soda cans could help your closet work twice as hard? Use a tab to hook two hangers together so you only have to hang one from the rod, saving valuable space for other organizers.

CATEGORIZE CLOTHES

One of the simplest methods for getting your closet into shape is to hang like items together, then sort each category by color. If you are really type A, you can even use your label maker to mark dividers.

DON'T FORGET THE DOOR

Rows of mini-baskets mounted inside a closet door offer lots of storage options for purses, belts, and socks, and make use of this often-ignored space.

DIVIDE AND CONQUER

Long closet shelves can easily fall into disarray as piles of clothes become jumbled together over time. Instead, invest in partitions. They clip or screw onto a shelf and divide it into compartments. Make the compartments as wide or narrow as needed to fit what you want to store.

JOY MANGANO HUGGABLE HANGERS®

Streamline and shrink your closet without tossing any pieces by swapping in Joy Huggable Hangers for mismatched plastic hangers. Slim to save space and flocked to keep items from slipping off, they are a must-have! Use multiple colors for even more organization.

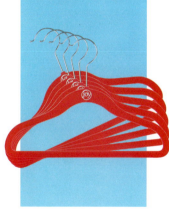

1-MINUTE TIP! **Keep clothes from slipping with rubber bands.** When a grippy rubber band meets a hanger, they become the ultimate (and cheapest) no-slip wardrobe organizer. No more shirts on the closet floor!

SEASONAL SUCCESS STRATEGIES

Follow these strategies each season for a happy, organized wardrobe.

DO A DOUBLE EDIT

Go through clothes and shoes from the season that just ended—remove anything stained, in need of repair, or worn out. Make a second pass through fall/winter clothes as you take them out of storage. Ask yourself, Did I wear this last winter? If not, was it because there was never the right occasion, or do you just not like it? Try on anything you're unsure about before giving it closet space.

ID TRANSITIONAL PIECES

For the first few weeks of any season, you may still want clothing options from the last season, especially if weather is unpredictable. Separate in-between pieces, like lightweight cardigans or a jean jacket. Then pack away things like sundresses, tank tops, and shorts, keeping chunky cold-weather options in storage until temperatures dip below 50°F.

CHANGE IT UP

Don't be afraid to make seasonal modifications to your closet setup to help it work better for fall's bulkier pieces. Temporary modular solutions, like a hanging sweater organizer, are a great way to add more shelf space.

SWITCH SHOES SEASONALLY

Drop off leather or suede boots at a shoe repair shop for cleaning, waterproofing, or new soles. You'll prolong their life, prep them for next year's messy winter weather, and save money in the long run.

GO SALE-ING!

Take note of any seasonal items that need to be replaced, like ratty jeans or beat-up leather sandals. If there's time, hit sales. Otherwise, put a shopping list inside the storage container so it'll be waiting for you when the seasons change again.

4 QUESTIONS FOR CLOTHES CLOSET DECLUTTERING

1 IS THE ARTICLE MORE THAN TWO SIZES TOO BIG OR TOO SMALL?

If so, give it away. Oversize clothes can be tailored down, but that can be costly, and there's no guarantee the lines will be the same. If you must lose a lot of weight to fit into a garment, decide if that's practical and worth hanging on to the item until then.

2 HAS IT BEEN MORE THAN ONE YEAR SINCE YOU'VE WORN THE PIECE?

Older pieces that aren't classics usually don't mix with newer ones. Just bite the bullet and donate them. The two exceptions: things that have high sentimental value, like a wedding dress, or luxury splurges you're hoping to pass down. Keep these, but relocate them to a lower traffic spot!

3 ARE THE CLOTHES IN BAD CONDITION?

If items are worn, frayed, or stained, discard or donate them. Just do it!

4 HAVE YOU CHANGED CAREERS OR STOPPED WORKING?

There may be clothes you no longer need. These are perfect to donate, especially if they are still in style and in good condition.

FAKE A SHOE CLOSET

Put your soles on display by lining up several tall (floor-to-ceiling tall!) shelving units (IKEA® Billy bookcases are just the right depth). Add a mirror nearby for last-minute outfit checks and arrange shoes by color so they are easy to find.

6 SMART IDEAS FOR SHOES AND BAGS

Because it's time to deal with that pile on the floor
of your closet once and for all!

1 GO BASIC. Start with a simple, inexpensive wire rack. It keeps footwear off the floor and is slanted at an angle so shoes are easy to find. For shelf storage, swap in clear plastic boxes for cardboard.

2 HELP BOOTS STAND TALL. Fight floppy boots and the mess they make of your closet floor with boot shapers. Cedar boot trees are great, but you can also DIY them using several paper towel or gift wrap rolls banded together, rolled-up magazines, or even repurposed pool noodles.

3 STASH MORE UNDER THE BED. If your closet is at max capacity, consider under-the-bed storage units. Most hold a dozen pairs of shoes or more, and ones on wheels are super-easy to roll in and out. Grab a few and dedicate them individually to heels, sandals, or flats.

4 ORGANIZE SHOES HEEL-TO-TOE. For closet storage in clear boxes, this easy trick gives you a quick look at everything—color, toe style, and heel height—so you'll never have to search for the perfect matching pair again.

5 STOCK YOUR SPARE PURSES. Running late to a wedding or work party? Leave easy-to-forget items (a mirror, business cards, and some cash) in your fave night-out bag or clutch. Just avoid things that could cause a mess, like makeup, hand cream, gum, and leaky pens. Store purses upright on a shelf with dividers.

6 HANG UP TOTES AND PURSES. Stop dropping your bag on the bed, chair, or (worse) the floor. Attach hooks to the inside of your closet door so everything has a place. This will make picking out a purse much easier.

1-MINUTE TIP! **Use shower curtain rings to hang scarves.** You can give all your colorful neck accessories individual attention when you loop shower curtain rings onto the crossbar of a hanger. This trick works for belts, too. Loosely knot slippery scarves to keep them from sliding to the floor.

CREATE A BUNK ROOM

Maximize sleeping spots for kids and their visitors with multiple built-in bunk beds. This trio is accented with industrial-pipe railings and a rope ladder that call to mind a dock or ship.

7 RULES FOR DECLUTTERING A KID'S ROOM—AND KEEPING IT THAT WAY

You'll need a strategy beyond just buying a ton of storage bins.

1 INVOLVE YOUR KIDS FROM THE BEGINNING. It's very important to work with them, not around them. Kids as young as three years old really want to participate and are excited to be involved. Plus, if kids are involved in organizing, they'll feel ownership over the project and be more inclined to keep things tidy—or, at the very least, they'll know where everything should go.

2 HAVE KIDS GIVE YOU A TOUR OF THE ROOM before you start decluttering. Don't start by asking kids to choose what should stay and what should go, give them a chance to look around and show you what's there. Get a sense of their language and tone, which can reveal things that are important to them and that they want to keep. Building that trust is important when asking kids to part with items. (Now you'll be able to tell more clearly what things they clearly don't care about.)

3 GIVE YOUR KIDS PERMISSION TO LET GO OF STUFF they really don't want. The sheer volume of their stuff can be overwhelming for children, but most kids don't know that it's OK to say no to stuff they no longer want. Try to set up situations in which you are donating items to charity—it continues the idea of using positive language when it comes to decluttering. Give the item a new home—don't just get rid of it.

4 START FROM THE BOTTOM UP— LITERALLY. With little ones, especially, it's just nice to start on the ground, since that's where they are. A "bottom up" strategy takes the process down to kids' level and keeps them grounded in the task. Plus, if they can see where their items' new homes are, they'll make a habit of placing them there.

5 REINFORCE THEIR ROUTINE WITH CUBBIES. A cubby is a great organizing tool for kids because it reinforces what they're experiencing at school. Place one in the entryway or their room to create a "drop zone" area they'll naturally maintain. With a cubby, kids can drop their stuff and not even have to think about it.

6 COUNT TO 10. Here's an easy fact to remember: Games are fun! So, when things get messy (as they always do), make cleaning up feel like play. Have kids count backward and pick up 10 items to put back in their homes at the end of the day. It makes the task less onerous and encourages you to talk out loud about where items go, which can reinforce the habit for both you and your kids.

7 LEAD BY EXAMPLE. You were probably waiting for this one, right? Leading by example is huge. Kids mirror what their parents are doing. Sometimes you need to look at yourself and really see if your kids are modeling your behavior. Even something as small as putting away your keys can be a mini-lesson in action.

TINY TWEAKS

Hang peel-and-stick wallpaper or a great
new mirror over the vanity for a speedy
refresh with huge style payoff. It can even
be as simple as changing up your drawer
pulls and streamlining the countertop
with stylish jars.

BATH + LAUNDRY ROOMS

Getting your ducks in a row in these hardworking spaces can streamline your whole life, not to mention your daily routine. In this chapter, we've got tricks to keep the frenzy at bay in your bathroom and laundry room, GH-style. Opt for our tried-and-tested advice to optimize every corner, including your medicine cabinet and linen closet. Dealing with tight quarters? Use our ingenious space-saving tricks. (Hint: See-through, acrylic bins are a life-saver!)

SPA-LIKE SANCTUARY

Chrome, marble, and calming white and gray are timeless in a master bathroom. Keep the counter clear and pretty by placing everyday items in apothecary jars. Instead of one giant mirror spanning a long vanity, hang one over each sink. Tuck towel racks in hidden places on either side of the vanity, and choose neutral tones for your towels, so they almost disappear.

Frame mirrors with sleek sconces.

STUNNING STYLE

Make a dramatic statement by mixing a dark vanity with brass hardware and white counters and walls. Choose a sink (or two!) that sits on top of the counter to score real drawer space below. Use shelves below for extra towels.

Mirrors enlarge any space but especially small ones like bathrooms.

PRO ORGANIZER TRICKS FOR ANY BATHROOM

Keep everything you need right at your fingertips—but off your countertops—with these ingenious ideas.

GO BIG

When your vanity lacks storage, it's time to improvise! Place a large woven basket under an open area to collect laundry or to house fresh towels. Then install a slim towel rack for hand towels and a deep medicine cabinet for daily-use items—anything to keep the counters clear and clutter-free!

SHELVE IT

Hang a tiered shelving unit above a freestanding tub to create a place to keep bath essentials and towels. Pretty it up with a display of supplies in artful packaging and glass jars.

GO OVER THE DOOR

Don't squander the valuable space hidden over your door. A towel rack or floating shelves can be easily installed there, creating a sleek bonus spot for bath essentials. Even one hook on the back of the door is better than nothing.

HAPPY HUTCH

This flexible piece of furniture works just as well in a bathroom as it does in any other room—and check out all the storage you get (glass-front cabinets let you easily see what's inside). Style it with pretty jars or trays and matching towels to keep the look neat and organized. Place a large basket on top for overflow items or extra toilet paper.

8 EASY WAYS TO CUT CLUTTER

Whether you have a small powder room or a sprawling master bath, make use of every inch with these terrific tips.

1 PUT CABINET DOORS TO WORK. Don't neglect the back of your cabinet doors. Keep flat irons, blow-dryers, and brushes close at hand but out of sight in special space-saving, mountable bins.

2 ADD EXTRA CABINETS. Your vanity is not your only option when it comes to bathroom cabinets. Mount one over the toilet or slip a tall, slim, freestanding one into the narrow space beside the toilet or sink. You'll be surprised at how much you can tuck inside and hide from view.

3 INSTALL SHELVES EVERYWHERE. Create extra storage where there once was none by adding rows of shelves. Have tall ceilings? Install a metal or wooden shelf about one foot from the ceiling. Fill the empty wall above the toilet or beside the shower with floating shelves, or consider a wall cabinet with a built-in towel bar.

4 PUT SLIDING DRAWERS UNDER THE SINK. Take advantage of all the room under your sink (and save yourself some stooping and reaching) with sliding drawers. Use them to store canisters with lids, which will keep essentials (like cotton balls or swabs) organized and fresh. Label each drawer so you know where everything is and where supplies should be returned when you're done with them.

5 HANG JARS OR BASKETS FOR VERTICAL STORAGE. A pallet is the perfect skinny surface from which to hang jars that house makeup tools. Plus, it acts as a design element first and storage second. Maximize even the smallest of walls with hanging baskets. Use them to stash extra supplies. Hang two above your toilet to hold rolled-up towels and discreetly hide toilet paper.

6 INSTALL MAGNETIC STRIPS. It's hard to fight the urge to toss bobby pins and tweezers into a cluttered pile. Outwit your laziness with a magnetic strip inside a medicine cabinet door or attached to a wall. These strips keep tools like tweezers, nail clippers, and mini-scissors neatly at hand and off the counter.

7 GET CREATIVE WITH TOWELS. Rods are best for hanging towels so they dry quickly and thoroughly, but they take up precious wall space. Instead, look for towel racks that hang from the back of the bathroom door or those with multiple swivel-out arms that mount in a corner.

8 CREATE YOUR OWN "SALON." Under the sink is the best spot for beauty necessities. Hang your hair dryer and curling iron on Command hooks inside the cabinet door. Then fill one side of the cabinet with elfa® drawers or other stackables to hold hairspray bottles, brushes, and more.

HOW TO DISPLAY
YOUR BATH ESSENTIALS

You use them every single day—now make them look pretty.

START WITH A GOOD PURGE

Shed expired and unused items, as well as bulky packaging. Leave everyday essentials—hand soap, toothbrushes—on the counter. Outfit cabinets with handy holders, such as a back-of-the-door rack.

CONTAIN IT

A shallow cabinet with sliding doors or a bar cart adds tons of storage in minimal space; trays and jars keep everything in order and woven baskets make shelves look neat, no matter what you throw in them.

TAME YOUR TOWELS

Stick to two sets per family member (assuming you do laundry once a week), plus two sets for guests. Consider Turkish towels, which take up less space than traditional terry cloth. Now there's more room for makeup!

THINK LIKE AN ARTIST

Style shelves or other display areas, like the window ledge, with your most beautiful lotions and potions. Line them up neatly in a row, collect them on a mirrored tray, or stack them pyramid-style.

PUT PERFUME ON A TRAY

A small decorative tray is the best way to contain and display your favorite scents. Not only does it keep them handy and ready to use, but the tray will protect your counter or shelving from drips or spills that might damage the finish.

1-MINUTE TIP! Streamline your shower.
Use an adjustable shower caddy to corral all your shower supplies in one spot—simplehuman® offers options with extendable necks and sliding shelves that can be customized to your daily routine. There are even spots to store products upside down so you get every last drop.

7 SMART SPACE-SAVERS

Maximize storage (no matter how limited your space is)
with these handy organizers.

1 SPICE RACK. The same organizers you use to hold spices are the perfect size for the equally small bottles in your adorable nail polish collection.

2 CLEAR, STACKABLE BINS. End the *Hmmm . . . what did I put in there?* mystery with lidded canisters in see-through acrylic. A multicompartment, transparent organizer herds together all those smaller, oddly shaped toiletries. Use these cheap-but-handy baskets to organize your drawers so everything from your morning routine has a home: cleansers, moisturizers, and makeup.

3 PORTABLE CADDY. A clear acrylic carry-all is a perfect spot to store beauty essentials or cleaning supplies. Get one with a handle so it's easy to pull out when you need it and put away when you don't.

4 FLOWERPOT. Use one with a saucer attached in the bathroom to hide and catch water drips from a plunger and in the garage to stash small garden tools.

5 LAZY SUSAN. Nothing's worse than having to hunt down your cleaning supplies when you're already in a rush to clean up before guests arrive. Use a Lazy Susan to make every product feel like it's front and center.

6 CLEVER SORTER. Make better use of the space on the back of the door by using an over-the-door organizing solution with slots for a hair-dryer nozzle and cords.

7 COMMAND HOOKS. All it takes are a couple of Command hooks to create a station on the side of your sink out of a wire container. Suddenly, your blow-dryer, curling iron, and straightener won't feel like they take up your entire vanity.

WALK-IN SHOWER

Skip a traditional door or curtain for a cleaner, more inviting look. Add a rack to one side for your everyday towel. Take advantage of the window ledge to corral bath soaps.

HANG A MIRROR

No need to cover up inconveniently placed windows or interesting wall designs. Instead, make the most of your "air rights" and suspend mirrors from the ceiling using pulleys and ropes.

10 THINGS YOU SHOULD REMOVE FROM YOUR BATHROOM RIGHT NOW

Time to find a new home for your makeup, jewelry, towels, and more.

1 BAR OF SOAP. Well, if you want to make cleaning this room easier, that is. Use a liquid soap with a pump or a hands-free soap dispenser to eliminate the need to clean a slimy soap dish or countertop every few days.

2 MEDICINE. Don't be fooled by your medicine cabinet: The bathroom is no place to store your meds, since it's prone to moisture and fluctuating temps. Instead, keep your prescriptions at room temperature in another room.

3 JEWELRY. The humid environment in the bathroom will speed up the oxidation process of your jewelry and cause it to tarnish—even if you don't wear it in the shower. You should keep precious items in a cool, dry room instead.

4 MAKEUP. It doesn't matter whether you wear powder, cream, or liquid makeup: All of it should be stored at room temp and therefore not in your bathroom. Hey, just add it to your list of reasons to invest in a new bedroom vanity.

5 PERFUME. Same goes for your perfume. Even though your first inclination might be to show off your pretty bottles in the room where you get ready—wait! Heat and humidity will cause your scent to spoil more quickly. Instead, showcase these lovely bottles in your bedroom or near a vanity.

6 NON-WATERPROOF ELECTRONICS. We get it: There's nothing like singing along to your favorite tunes in the shower. But the high humidity makes technology that isn't designed for the bathroom vulnerable to damage. Our advice: Pick out a waterproof device to be safe.

7 LINENS. Since bathrooms often breed mold and mildew, keep linens, like towels and sheets, in another room. Running the exhaust fan as much as possible can also help to air out damp towels after your shower.

8 BOOKS AND MAGAZINES. It's tempting to keep your bathroom reading material nearby, but the humidity mixed with the paper will damage your favorite reads, so when they're not in use, keep them in a dry place instead.

9 NAIL POLISH. Even though these pretty colors have a life expectancy of two years, if you keep them in the bathroom with its always-fluctuating temperatures, they may not last that long. Instead, keep them in a place that stays at room temperature, like your bedroom.

10 EXTRA RAZORS. Your current blade can stay safely stashed in your shower or medicine cabinet, but keep the others in another room. Why? The moisture and steam from the shower might dull or rust your blades before you get a chance to use them!

157

MEDICINE CABINET MAKEOVERS

Follow these tricks to keep it from becoming the "junk drawer" of the bathroom.

CLEAR OUT

Take everything out and give the inside a good cleaning. Toss any out-of-date cosmetics or those you've tried and decided weren't quite right. Bring expired or unwanted medications to your local police station for proper disposal.

SORT BY A.M. VERSUS P.M.

Put lotions, potions, and skin-care essentials on two different shelves—one for morning, one for night. Or group like items together; that is, place everything that has to do with dental care (floss, toothpaste, mouthwash) in one area and all your hair styling aids in another.

ADD ORGANIZERS

Deck out shelves with lidded acrylic canisters—they're excellent for holding cotton swabs and applicators and won't shatter if they tumble out.

RELOCATE THE SPACE-WASTERS

If you have things stored in your medicine cabinet that are not used daily, move them to another location in the bathroom. That includes seldom-used fragrances, surplus cosmetics, and first-aid supplies, which will feel more at home in a clearly labeled container under the sink or in a more spacious cabinet.

MAGNETIZE THE DOOR

Install magnetic strips (typically used for kitchen knives) to hold small tools like nail clippers, tweezers, and an eyelash curler.

MOVE YOUR MEDS

Take over-the-counter medicines and prescriptions out of the bathroom (humidity breaks them down) and place them in a hall closet or pantry where the temperature is more stable.

VICKS® VAPORUB™ Stock this topical ointment in your medicine cabinet. It helps relieve coughing due to colds, thanks to its blend of camphor, eucalyptus, and menthol.

STREAMLINE YOUR MAKEUP

Most of us have makeup collections that could use a serious purge.
Read on for our expert tips on when to throw away what.

- **EVERY SEASON**
  Toss mascara and liquid eye or lip liner.

- **EVERY SIX MONTHS**
  Toss skin-care products, sunscreens, and liquid foundation.

- **EVERY YEAR**
  Toss hair-care products (except hair spray).

- **EVERY TWO YEARS**
  Toss powder-based cosmetics (such as pressed powder and eye shadows), lipsticks, fragrances, and nail polish.

WHAT IS THE DEAL WITH "NATURAL" PRODUCTS?
They may have an extra-short shelf life because their botanical ingredients (think pure extract, oil, pulp, rind, tree bark, fruits, or leaves) may be susceptible to microbial growth.

WHAT ABOUT THINGS THAT ARE STILL IN THE PACKAGING?
Unopened, well-formulated cosmetics can remain stable for a couple of years at room temperature. The clock starts once you open it. When air hits the formula, certain ingredients start to oxidize and degrade. What's more, every time you touch your makeup or skin-care products, you transfer germs to them—and, subsequently, to your face. Heat and humidity, which promote the growth of mold and yeast, are factors, too. That's one reason the bathroom, though convenient, isn't the ideal spot to store cosmetics. A better place: a cool, dry linen closet.

TIGHT-SPACE TRICKS

Open shelves encourage people to keep towels and toiletries neat, and built-in cubbies save precious floor space. A small wastebasket keeps things tidier because it gets emptied more often. And a custom-sized, recessed shelf in the shower is a sleek way to keep shampoo and conditioner in order and within easy reach.

FAKE A LINEN CLOSET

Create a designated space for towels and bathing essentials—inside or outside the bathroom—with a set of tall shelves. Put it on wheels so it's easy to move. Place a decorative mirror or a piece of art on top for a finished look.

6 TRICKS FOR ORGANIZING A CHAOTIC LINEN CLOSET

Items of all shapes and sizes inhabit this space. Here's how to make sure yours is neat and tidy.

1 ADD STORAGE TO THE DOOR. Install hooks or a few horizontal towel racks to the back of the door to stash extra sets of towels, tablecloths, blankets, shower curtains—or even your robe—and free up shelf space for other necessities.

2 USE A MIX OF CONTAINERS. Choose clear containers with lids so toilet tissue, first aid supplies, and extra toiletries stay clean and at hand. Trays are perfect to corral small items that might otherwise get lost. Square wire baskets with cotton inserts and pretty labels keep cleaning supplies in order.

3 OPTIMIZE TOWEL FOLDING. Not all shelves are the same size—some are wider and some deeper. Fold your towels to fit on the appropriate-size shelves and end the toppling, or roll and stack them so it's easier to grab one at a time. You can also separate sections with metal dividers and use labels to designate what goes where.

4 STASH SHEETS IN PILLOWCASES. Place all items from one set—flat and top sheets and remaining pillowcases—neatly inside one case. This way, an entire set comes out with just one tug, and you'll never end up with unmatched pillowcases.

5 DESIGNATE AND DIVIDE SHELVES. Establish order by allocating specific items to each shelf—bath necessities, guest-room bedding, etc. Add custom dividers on each shelf to further keep items from migrating where they don't belong.

6 RELOCATE THE EXTRAS. Buying in bulk or taking advantage of a great sale on toilet paper or new sheets is cost-effective but can quickly translate into linen closet mayhem. Reorganize this space to ensure it's well-stocked with things you use regularly, then move all the stuff you don't need to a less high-traffic area.

1-MINUTE TIP! **Assess the contents.** The linen closet can easily become a dumping ground for old and ratty towels or incomplete bedding sets that you'll never use again. Avoid this by pulling out a stack of towels or sheets, and look for frayed edges, holes, bleach spots, or missing pieces. If you find anything that has seen better days, get it out of there!

COUNTER THAT

Frame a front-load washer and dryer with an easy-to-clean countertop to score much-needed folding space. Upper cabinets can hide all your laundry basics. A large basket will come in handy when emptying the machines.

PRO TIPS FOR AN ORDERED LAUNDRY ROOM

The more streamlined and functional this area is, the more quickly you can get the job done!

CREATE EXTRA WORKSPACE

You may not have room for a cart, full cabinet, or extra piece of furniture, but you probably have space for a shelf. Even a short one, hung at counter height, will offer a handy extra surface for sorting, folding, or placing items as you load and unload the machines.

PUT THE UGLY STUFF IN DECORATIVE BINS

Detergent bottles and dryer sheet boxes will fade into the background when placed in woven baskets. Make sure they are out of reach and out of sight of little ones.

PAINT THE ROOM A PLEASANT COLOR

Decorating a utility space feels frivolous, but think about how much time you actually spend in there. A serene wall color will make you happier and more likely to keep things orderly.

MAXIMIZE SHELVING

Easy access to all your laundry-day tools and products is key, so embrace open shelving. Stocky, clean shelves, hung in pairs, will always look tidier than a wire rack or an unfinished plank, and they can show off decorative vessels used to hold spare change, extra buttons, clothespins, and other laundry essentials.

TRY A WALL-MOUNTED DRYING RACK

Space-saving and functional, a rack like those from Polder® expands when you need it and disappears when you don't. Hang it over a sink for drip-drying.

TIDE® ORIGINAL HE TURBO CLEAN

This detergent not only cleans and removes stains, but also has quick-collapsing suds to keep high-efficiency washers working their best.

SORTING STATION

If you can, place a table in your laundry room to organize clean laundry. Assign a basket or bin to each family member or room so clean laundry makes it to the right place. Fold and put away clean laundry within 24 hours to keep from mixing freshly washed and dirty clothes.

8 WAYS TO MASTER LAUNDRY MESS

Take control of those piles of dirty clothes with these ingenious ideas.

1 SORT AT THE SOURCE. Place a double hamper or baskets for dirty clothes—one for lights and whites, one for darks—in each family member's bedroom. Come laundry day, it will cut down on sorting time so you can get loads washed faster.

2 DO A POCKET CHECK. Before depositing clothes in the washer, empty out change, receipts, gum, etc. into a clear jar. Stash used dryer sheets in another jar (they make great dust wipes and, tucked into shoes, effective odor stoppers).

3 STOP SPILLS. Prevent sticky drips by storing liquid cleaners on rimmed trays out of kids' reach. And consider streamlining—one all-purpose detergent, chlorine and nonchlorine bleach, and a pretreater should do.

4 TACKLE SPOTS—NOW! The sooner you do, the better your chances of getting them out. Immediately apply a stain remover and soak the item of clothing in a basin of sudsy water if you aren't washing it right away. Look for stain removers, like Shout® Advanced Action Gel, that can be safely applied to fabrics up to one week before washing.

5 ORGANIZE THE EXTRAS. Keep supplies—like linen water for a scent boost, lint rollers, and spray starch for sharp collars—together in a caddy. You're more likely to use them if they're on hand and sorted.

6 RACK THEM UP. Instead of perching your clothing-care tools wherever you can, install organizers, such as a wall-mounted iron and an ironing-board holder.

7 HANG THEM OUT TO DRY. If you're pressed for space, hang wall- or door-mounted racks to give wet clothes room to dry. Or, put up a closet rod or a retractable clothesline above the washer/dryer for damp blouses and delicates. Room to spare? Install pull-out drying racks made of mesh fabric, PVC pipe, and drawer sliders.

8 REPURPOSE THE TOPS. A surface for fluffing and folding can help you keep clean clothes from piling up. If you don't have a built-in counter, create one yourself by laying a piece of cut-to-fit butcher block atop your washer and dryer.

HOW TO SORT THE RIGHT WAY

Follow these steps to keep colors bright and fabrics damage-free.

START WITH COLORS

Clothes with deep hues are more likely to release dye, so group them together. If you have something you think may bleed (apply a drop of water and dab with a white paper towel to check), wash it separately the first few times.

MOVE ON TO FABRIC

Separate lint "givers" from lint "receivers." That means towels and wool sweaters shouldn't be washed or dried along with corduroy or velour. It's also best to keep fabrics of similar weight together so that coarse fabrics won't abrade and pill delicates and everything will finish drying at the same time.

FINISH WITH SOIL LEVEL

Very dirty or stained laundry needs more attention (more detergent or a longer, more aggressive cycle) than lightly soiled fabrics do. Sorting by dirt level will keep cleaner items from getting dirtier.

TABLE UP

Place a long, slim, console table beside the front door to drop mail, keys, and newspapers. Large woven baskets and decorative baskets keep things pretty and organized. Turn the table into a stylish vignette by hanging a pair of mirrors above it.

ENTRYWAYS, GARAGES + MORE

Boots, coats, gloves, umbrellas—all things that can easily make any entryway look as though a hurricane just touched down. Whether it's the front door or the mudroom, this space gives a peek into just how orderly the rest of your house is, so if you want to spend extra time in particular areas, be sure to do it here. From the beauty of catchall baskets to well-placed hooks and speed-cleaning tips, here's how to create the warmest welcome.

PRO ORGANIZER TRICKS TO STEAL

Bring order and calm to the most high-traffic zones in your home with these simple switches.

MINI-PERCH

Slip a slim bench by the door, so your family and guests have a place to put on and remove footwear—or temporarily toss a jacket or mail. Tuck a large basket below the bench for shoes and other outdoor staples, and style it with a couple pretty cushions.

GO FOR AN ARMOIRE

No closet? No problem. Give an old armoire a new coat of paint, add shelf paper and a hanging rod, and stock it with hangers for all your coats and jackets. Use the drawers below for hats, scarves, and other outdoor accessories.

MIX SHELVES AND CUBBIES

Opt for storage cubbies or built-ins
that boast open bases, so shoes can be
kicked off and stored underneath without
creating a traffic pileup. Organizational
must-haves, like hooks and baskets, make
arrivals (and departures) a cinch.

USE EVERY NOOK

Don't let a single surface go unused. A large hook on a narrow piece of wall by the door is ideal to hang grab-and-go essentials, like a dog-supply bag or purse. Turn a tiny half-height wall into a mini-library, and fill an empty corner at the base of the stairs with a collectibles table.

ELEVATE YOUR ENTRY

There's nothing inviting about a foyer that's become a de facto dumping ground. Here's how to help your home make a great first impression!

PUT OUT THE WELCOME MATS

Place doormats outside and inside doors to trap dirt. Add a boot tray to encourage all guests and family members to remove shoes and keep tracked-in dirt and scuffs off floors. These simple steps go a long way to eliminating virtually all the tracked-in dirt that can wreak havoc on a wood floor's finish. Dirt and grit are abrasive, and over time, these particles leave behind fine scratches that make your floors look dull.

HANG AN UP-HIGH SHELF

Taking advantage of unused overhead space is a great way to keep items you don't use every day out of the way. Neutral bins on shelves turn clutter into a decorative accent.

REPURPOSE A HAMPER

It's helpful to have a covered bin where you can toss things without thinking twice. Keep everything from soccer balls to other yard games out of sight.

GO MONOCHROME

An all-white look might not be everyone's cup of tea, but choosing just one hue imparts a neat-and-tidy aesthetic, even when things get a little cluttered.

MAKE ROOM FOR A BENCH

If you have a place to sit and put your shoes on, or a seat to prop your purse while you remove your coat, it can help you feel less frazzled both entering and leaving your house. Then, you'll be less likely to toss your bag wherever it lands when you're crouched on the floor untying your sneakers.

MANAGE MAIL AND KEYS

Set up a mail station with trays or a wall-mounted caddy and keep only what needs immediate attention here—along with stamps, pens, and a notepad. File, recycle, or shred the rest. Place keys in a central location, either on hooks or in a dish, so you'll always know where to find them.

SORT AND STOW

A table or bench with separate bins lets you stash recycling, shoes, and more right by the door. Or, give each family member his or her own basket.

MAXIMIZE YOUR MUDROOM

Bring a sense of order and style to the busiest room in the house.

1 ORGANIZE WITH TRAYS AND FAKE BUILT-INS. Just as a tray on a coffee table helps contain things, so do boot trays on a mudroom floor. Set out two or three near the door to keep shoes and boots from piling up. Line them with garden pebbles or stones to allow wet footwear to dry without standing in a puddle. Yesterday's newspaper will also do the job.

2 CONSIDER A COATRACK. A freestanding coatrack is a great small-space solution and easy way to accommodate extra coats, hats, and scarves. But keep in mind that a coatrack can topple under the weight of heavy coats, so use it for items that can't be stored in an existing closet.

3 DESIGNATE SHELVES FOR SPECIFIC THINGS. If you've got a newborn, pets, or kids in the house, dedicate areas in your mudroom for their on-the-go essentials. For a baby, think diaper-bag necessities, wipes, and changing pads. Always keep pet leashes and treats in one spot.

4 HANG MORE HOOKS. You might never have success getting the kids to regularly and consistently hang their coats in a closet, but the barrier to entry for a hook is low. And jackets look much neater along a wall than piled on your couch. Install hooks in a straight line near the door. For best results, try one or two hooks per family member (including pets).

5 BE STRATEGIC WITH BINS. Deep baskets are perfect for corralling your family's sneaker collection or other random sports gear (items that don't necessarily need to stay pristine). Hang smaller baskets for odds and ends like keys or sunglasses that you often grab at the last minute on your way out the door.

6 HAVE FUN WITH DÉCOR. Cute accents aren't required in a functional space, but every part of your home should make you happy. Playful décor, like a fun carpet in a mudroom, adds levity to utilitarian spots. Use durable, inexpensive FLOR tiles that can be tailored to your floor plan.

7 ELIMINATE A CRAMMED CLOSET. Getting rid of a fully loaded closet may seem like a sacrilege to any homeowner bursting at the seams with stuff, but it can be a smart way to go. More open space gives you storage flexibility (and may offer family members more room as they're running out the door).

8 MAKE SPACE FOR FIDO. Assign a special bin or drawer or a dedicated wall hook for leashes, a flashlight for nighttime walks, puppy sweaters or coats, and a cloth for wiping wet paws. Keep a stash of waste bags, a fur brush, and a pet-hair remover (for your clothes and upholstery) in this space, too.

GARDENING GEAR PROBLEMS SOLVED! If you're an avid gardener and like to put your garden togs on as you go out the door, the mudroom is a logical place to keep your favorite gardening shirt, clogs, kneepads, and apron. Garden footwear should be kept on a simple shoe rack that is easy to clean. Keep other gardening apparel in a bin or attractive basket on a shelf or the floor by the back door. When gardening season is over, clean all garments, gardening gloves, and footwear, and tuck them away in a lidded, labeled storage tote in your basement or garage.

HOW TO MAXIMIZE STORAGE IN YOUR BASEMENT OR ATTIC

STICK WITH THE RIGHT STUFF

These bonus spaces are still a must-have for many homeowners. Use them to stash items like holiday decorations, kitchen supplies (including infrequently used pots, pans, serving dishes, and plates), suitcases, and patio furniture. Put whatever you can in airtight containers, especially in the basement.

BE SMART WITH SHELVES

Add as much floor-to-ceiling shelving as possible. Shelves that are at least a foot off the floor are ideal. Use stackable, hard-plastic, see-through containers (with lids!) instead of cardboard boxes.

LABEL EVERYTHING

Even if you follow our advice and use see-through plastic containers, it's still important to clearly label each box. Label each side and the top, so no matter how the box is stored, you can clearly read what's inside.

BE AWARE OF MOISTURE

Climate control is key. Run a dehumidifier/humidifier, if necessary. Just the humidity in the air can cause items to smell musty or damage wooden furniture. A humidity level of 40–50 percent is ideal.

5 THINGS YOU SHOULD NEVER STORE IN YOUR BASEMENT OR ATTIC

During a big move or organizing project, it's tempting to stash boxes in out-of-the-way spots. But if you want your stuff to survive, you need to be careful about what you place in these spaces that are neither climate- nor pest-controlled.

1 DELICATE FABRICS. Mice, insects, temperature fluctuations, and water damage are all reasons to keep these in a closet instead. And beware: Even your beloved summer linen pants or cotton sweaters—not just your wool—are prone to moth infestation. Fur and leather need a reliably cool climate to keep looking their best. Vintage pieces, wedding gowns, sentimental baby clothing, and fine linens should all be cleaned and packaged by a professional cleaner, then kept in the main part of the house.

2 FURNITURE AND DÉCOR MADE FROM NATURAL MATERIALS. Wood and upholstered furniture don't belong in the attic, basement, or garage. Wood mildews (you can try to bleach it, but you may have to toss it). Area rugs, mattresses, and even plush toys are too susceptible to moisture damage to hold up in the face of temperature and humidity fluctuations for very long. They all need dry, moderate temperatures for proper storage, and dampness from humidity or water leakage is a problem for everything. It ruins items and promotes mold growth.

3 IMPORTANT PAPERS. Birth certificates, passports, marriage licenses, and school and medical records don't belong in boxes where they could become wet or illegible. If important papers must be filed in the basement, put them in plastic containers up on a shelf. But using a safe or closet is a much better alternative. The same holds true for photos, books, and artwork, which can be ruined by moisture and extreme heat. If they're not properly stored, they can suffer discoloration, staining, or even mold.

4 FOOD (UNLESS STORED CAREFULLY). If you use your basement for provisions other than root vegetables, make sure to put them in airtight canisters. In fact, pack perishables in airtight plastic bags before placing them in hard-plastic containers to ward off insects and discourage mildew and rot.

5 ANYTHING ELECTRONIC OR FLAMMABLE. Paints, turpentine, cleaning products, gasoline, propane, kerosene, or other hazardous chemicals should never be located near anything gas-related (the furnace, water heater, dryer, fireplace, or a stove or oven) or stored in the attic, which tends to get very warm. Extreme heat and moisture can wreck even the most well-made electronics.

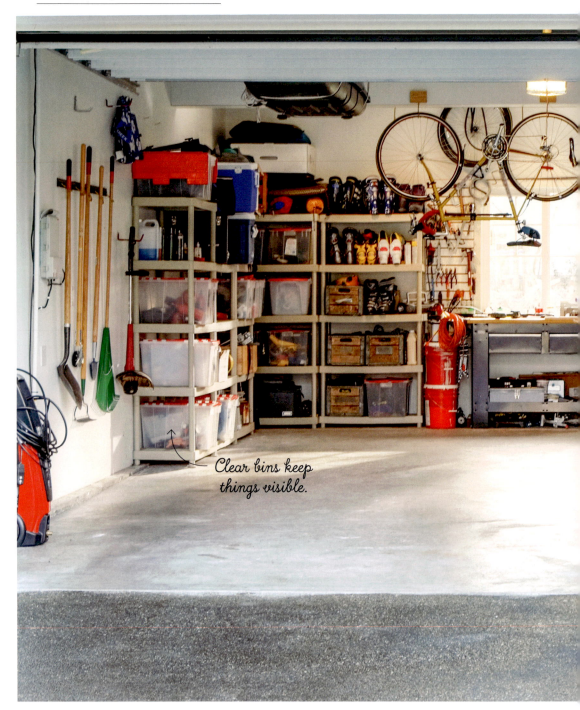

Clear bins keep things visible.

8 SPACE-SAVING STRATEGIES FOR THE GARAGE

Don't forget this all-important area—you may even make room for the car.

1 MAKE A WORKSPACE. Set up an area in your garage for DIY projects and repairs. Select a surface, whether it's a counter-height table, a rolling cart with wheel locks, or a set of sawhorses topped with a board. Mount a pegboard so tools are within reach. Add a stool and task lamp and you're all set.

2 SEE WHAT YOU'VE GOT. Group similar items and determine the best bin or box size for each group. Stow extension cords, rags, and other bulky items in wire baskets for visibility, then tuck them under a countertop or up on a shelf. Store bigger baskets with heavier items in low places and smaller, lighter baskets higher up.

3 ADD WALL HOOKS. Another great way to free up floor space is to add a row of customizable wall hooks. (Check out the options at your local hardware or building-supply store.) Use them to hang rakes, lawn chairs, hoses, extension cords, and other outdoor essentials.

4 HANG WHAT YOU CAN. Free up precious counter and floor space with one or more wall-mounted rails for hanging frequently used items. Even big items, like garden hoses and wheelbarrows, can be stowed on well-anchored pegboards next to rakes and hand tools. Secure them with heavy-duty bungee cords.

5 STICK 'EM UP. Store hand tools in cleaned-up soup cans or mason jars so they are contained but easy to find and grab.

6 GET LABELING. Limit rummaging by providing clear descriptions (e.g., CAMPING GEAR), especially for items stowed in opaque, lidded totes.

7 BUILD HIGH, NOT WIDE. Wall-hung cabinets and shelving systems allow for vertical storage and take advantage of wall space. Loft-like storage options, such as wooden shelves or easily installed rack units, are ideal for holding seasonal items like outdoor gear. Rotate out boxes or bins as needed (don't forget to label them). Pack supplies in plastic storage bins when possible to keep out dust, moisture, and grime.

8 PUT UP PEGBOARDS. They're great for hanging tools, from rakes to screwdrivers. Find one at a hardware store, then paint it and draw an outline around each item with permanent marker to make cleanup straightforward. A magnetic knife strip is perfect for holding small metal tools, nails, and screws.

HOW TO STORE DANGEROUS GOODS Keep toxic solvents, cleaners, and chemicals in a well-ventilated, lockable cabinet to protect against prying hands and careless spills. Make sure they're in tightly sealed containers, away from heat or flames. Put a clipboard inside with an ever-sharp pencil attached to keep a record of the contents and how long you've had each product.

HAND AND POWER TOOL STORAGE

Think safety first as you corral and declutter.

SET UP A DIY PROJECT AREA

First, select a surface: a counter-height table, rolling cart with wheel locks, or set of sawhorses topped with a countertop or board. Mount a pegboard over your surface to hang supplies. Add an adjustable-height stool, sturdy task lamp, and small fan to keep you cool and dissipate any fumes.

BOX ESSENTIALS

Every home should have a basic tool kit stored in a small, portable toolbox. Look for one with sturdy handles and small utility drawers to hold a few screws, nails, and washers. Is your tool collection extensive? Choose a larger standing or rolling toolbox with a variety of drawers of different depths, attached cabinets, and open shelves.

PROTECT CORDS

If your power tool has a cord, use heavy-duty twist ties to keep it in a tidy loop. Never hang a tool by its power cord; you may damage it and make the tool unsafe to use.

HANG IT UP

Too busy to set up your own pegboard? Invest in custom-perforated panels with hanging pins made to support small tools plus special accessories, like hanging chisel trays and screwdriver racks. Or, keep hand tools in hanging cabinets attached to wall studs, which allows you to lock them up.

KEEP CASES

The majority of power tools come with their own hard-plastic carrying case, and they are often sold in complete sets with extra blades or bits right inside. If you have an older power tool without a container, buy a carrying case to accommodate the tool and accessories—and stay organized.

SHELVE THEM

For safety—and because they're expensive—you may want to store power tools in a closed and locked cabinet (along with hand tools), if you have children. Dedicate different shelves for different types of tools, such as those for cutting, drilling, and shaping.

1-MINUTE TIP! **Outline zones.** Use painter's tape or masking tape on the floors or walls to mark where various types of belongings go. Store things on wheels, like toy cars or bicycles, as far away from parking spots as possible to avoid inadvertent dings.

SEASONAL SUPPLIES

Items that you take out once a year must
be handy when you want them and out of
sight when you don't. A garage, attic, or
basement provides ample storage space.
Be extra careful with items that have high
sentimental value.

STORING HOLIDAY DECORATIONS

Be ready for the festivities year after year with these simple tips.

VILLAGE SETS

For decorations that are displayed together, such as nativity sets, holiday villages, or train sets, be sure to store the individual pieces together. If possible, keep such items in their original packaging. That way, you'll know they're protected and will easily spot them next year.

ORNAMENTS

Tuck small ornaments in cleaned-out egg cartons. Instead of tossing out used tissue paper with the recycling, use it as extra packing material to cushion ornaments in containers. Cardboard dividers (make your own from cut-up cereal boxes or shoeboxes) will also buffer delicate glass. Decorations made with dried food should be stored in airtight containers to protect them from pests or moisture.

BLOW-UP ITEMS

Inflatable decorations displayed outside should be cleaned before storing. While Santa's inflated, wipe the nylon fabric with a damp cloth and allow it to dry before deflating and storing. If necessary, use a mild detergent to get rid of winter dirt.

CANDLES

Never place candles in a box in the garage or the attic. If an area's temperature gets too hot, the candles could soften and warp. Instead, wrap them in white tissue paper or bubble wrap to keep them from getting nicked and chipped, and tuck them into an out-of-the-way spot in the main part of the house.

SPECIAL SORTERS

There are a multitude of specialty organizers and covers on the market for lights, wreaths, trees, ornaments, and even gift wrap. Large plastic totes come color-coded for easily telling Halloween decorations from Christmas ones and can fit nicely on basement, attic, or garage shelves. This is often the easiest way to keep these infrequently used items organized and protected.

BE READY FOR NEXT YEAR

After storing all your decorations, create or refill your holiday décor emergency kit with ornament hooks and hangers, tacks, and replacement holiday lightbulbs, often on sale immediately after the holidays.

EASY WAYS TO ORGANIZE YOUR OUTDOOR STUFF

Keeping indoor spaces tidy is tough, but outdoor gear presents special challenges. Here's help.

THE GRILL

- If you don't have a grill cover, now's the time to get and use one. Secure it snugly to the grill so it doesn't blow off.

- Give the grill grates a good cleaning outside before packing the grill away, and don't forget to empty and clean the grease drip tray so it doesn't attract animals during storage. For charcoal grills, clean out and safely dispose of any leftover charcoal ash.

- Never store propane tanks indoors. If you want to store a grill indoors, remove the propane tank and store it separately.

SPORTS EQUIPMENT

- Corral small sports gear, like bats, balls, and hockey sticks, in a go-to bin in the garage so family members can drop off or pick up things while passing through.

- You can buy individual hangers that keep snowboards or skis in place, but it usually makes more sense to purchase units integrated with shelving and hooks for boots and poles.

- Tuck bikes and scooters below wall-mounted shelves or suspend them from a garage ceiling or wall so they don't take up floor space or fall over. The most basic types of hanging systems are coated wall hooks that support the frame of the bike. More advanced ones include bike trees that can store the bike horizontally or vertically, depending on available space. If you have lots of overhead clearance, consider a bike pulley system—the bike is mounted on suspended supports and then hoisted overhead and out of the way.

- Multisport organizers are a great choice if your family tends to play many different ball sports, such as baseball, tennis, and basketball, or if you have a lot of small accessories to store, such as kneepads and helmets for skateboarding. The organizer usually combines a large bin for loose balls and other items; hanging slots and hooks for bats and racquets; a shelf or small hangers for gloves, caps, and helmets; and additional storage accessories, such as small bins.

OUTDOOR FURNITURE AND TOYS

- At season's end, move patio furniture to the garage, shed, or a covered area, if possible. For pieces too big to store indoors, protect them with covers. Make sure to secure the covers to the furniture so they don't blow away.

- Consider a weather-resistant deck box if you have lots of pillows and cushions to store. Not only does it work off-season to hold these space-hogging items, but it also makes it easier to protect them from rain showers all summer long. Protecting them when they're not in use keeps them looking newer longer.

- Cover large outdoor toys, like a playhouse, sandbox, or water table, with a tarp and secure each one with a bungee cord.

HOW TO STORE GAS SAFELY Keep fuel for gas-powered tools locked up in a metal cabinet to prevent accidents. Always empty fluids from seasonal equipment (such as a snowblower or lawn mower) for off-season storage.

Shelves add more counter space.

7 TRICKS FOR YARD-CARE TOOLS

Here's how to keep them clean, tidy, and ready for work.

1 MAKE ROOM FOR MOWERS. If you have a lawn mower with a folding handle, always fold it up and position it out of the way. Lawn-mower accessories, such as a grass-catcher bag, should be cleaned out after each use and hung up to keep the mess out of your storage area.

2 HANG LONG-HANDLED TOOLS. Never leave rakes, shovels, hoes, etc., leaning against a wall. Simply hammer large penny nails into a wall or stud. Leave room for the tool handle between the nails, then hang the shovel or rake upside down, with nails supporting its head.

3 LABEL PLANTS NOW FOR SPEEDY ID-ING LATER ON. Use green labels for what's edible and red for what isn't. Also, stop bugs from sneaking into pot drainage holes by cutting out squares from screens and placing them in pot bottoms.

4 WRAP UP GARDEN HOSES. Wind them into a hose caddy on wheels, an attractive hose bowl, or a metal hose reel (wall-mounted or stationary).

5 USE A BUCKET CADDY. This portable, multipurpose organizer is made of a tool belt attached to a five-gallon plastic bucket. Take the tools and bucket wherever you go in your garden. So handy!

6 STACK POTS AND PLANTERS NEATLY. Store them close to potting supplies. Keep plastic planters out of direct sunlight, as too much exposure can crack and fade plastic pots and boxes.

7 SHELVE YOUR SUPPLIES. Stack bagged supplies, such as mulch, or store them in tubs to prevent leakage. Keep loose supplies (fertilizer spikes, seed packets) in trays with labels.

4 MORE WAYS TO MAKE SPACE

1 TRY A MINI-BENCH.
Look for slim seating that fits neatly against any wall. Top it with succulents to add a layer of decoration, and stow them underneath when entertaining a larger crowd.

2 DO MORE WITH FURNITURE.
Turn a workbench into a friendly display for greenery and other knickknacks. The lower shelf stores firewood out of the way, and the top acts as a buffet during summer potlucks.

3 HANG BISTRO LIGHTS.
The warm glow from these lights instantly turns a cramped patio into a cozy one. Here, bulbs get an extra cute punch from patterned pennants.

4 ADD A CHARMING WINDOW BOX.
It requires minimal room, and you can enjoy it whether you're inside or outside. Use it to plant bright flowers or fresh herbs, like basil, parsley, and rosemary.

VERTICAL GARDEN

When you run out of yard space, create a potted plant organizer out of plywood planks and a stepladder painted a bright color.

BONUS "ROOMS"

Add pillows, colorful throws, and cozy furniture to turn a back deck or patio into an extension of your indoor space. Use an outdoor rug to define the space and make it feel even more like an al fresco living room.

HOW TO DECLUTTER YOUR CAR

Count on these six solutions to clean your wheels in 15 minutes or less—and keep your ride in tip-top shape.

SORT AND TOSS

Grab two small trash bags and an empty box. Start at the front and move to the rear (look under the seats!), tossing trash into one bag. Anything that belongs in the house (like that stray lipstick tube) goes in the other bag. What stays in the car goes into the box.

TACKLE TRUNK JUNK

Sort everything from groceries to clothing headed for the cleaners by organizing your trunk with collapsible bins. Keep them in place by attaching the bristled part of Velcro tape to the bottom—it'll stick to the fuzzy lining of your trunk and prevent sliding.

TAME CORDS

Messy cords and cables can be an eyesore—and are dangerous if they slip beneath your feet when you're driving. Neaten them by putting a phone holder in a cup holder, then use Command Cord Clips to secure wires and chargers.

FIND A HOME

For the items that stay: A visor organizer is perfect for stuff like favorite CDs. Put maps in a large resealable bag in the driver's side cubby; manuals and registration documents go in the glove compartment. Use an empty pill bottle to store coins for tolls; keep it handy in a cup holder.

UNCLUTTER THE BACKSEAT

Use an organizer like Back Pockets for toys, ice scrapers, umbrellas, etc. Put emergency car supplies, like jumper cables and flares, in an empty toolbox that you keep in the trunk.

BE PREPARED

Head off trash accumulation: Fill an empty tissue box with plastic bags from the grocery store and stash it under the front seat. Then you're ready to roll.

SPEEDY 2-STEP CLEANUP

1 SWIPE. Clean the dashboard, doorjambs, armrests, and steering wheel with Armor All® Cleaning Wipes, which handle grime without harming vinyl or leather. Or use ordinary baby wipes, which are tough but gentle.

2 SHAKE & VACUUM. Remove and shake out the floor mats. Using a handheld vacuum—we like the Eureka® 71A, which comes with a stretch hose—go over the seats and the floor. Treat spills and ink spots with hand sanitizer; its high alcohol content zaps stains. Slip the mats back in.

FEBREZE CAR VENT CLIPS Keep your car smelling fresh, no matter how old it is, with these easy-to-use clips. Just attach them to your car's vents, then choose either a light or more intense scent via the control dial on the top.

PHOTO CREDITS

INDEX

HEARSTBOOKS

An Imprint of Sterling Publishing Co., Inc.
1166 Avenue of the Americas
New York, NY 10036

ISBN 978-1-61837-278-9

Distributed in Canada by Sterling Publishing
c/o Canadian Manda Group, 664 Annette Street
Toronto, Ontario M6S 2C8, Canada
Distributed in Australia by NewSouth Books
University of New South Wales, Sydney, NSW 2052, Australia

For information about custom editions, special sales, and premium and corporate purchases, please contact Sterling Special Sales at 800-805-5489 or specialsales@sterlingpublishing.com.

Manufactured in China

2 4 6 8 10 9 7 5 3 1

sterlingpublishing.com
goodhousekeeping.com

Cover design by Scott Russo
Interior design by Susan Welt
For photo credits, see page 194